# CARY GRANT

# CARY GRANT

*Pyramid Illustrated History of the Movies*

by
## JERRY VERMILYE

*General Editor:* **TED SENNETT**

PUBLICATIONS
NEW YORK

**CARY GRANT**
**Pyramid Illustrated History of the Movies**

CARY GRANT
*Pyramid Illustrated History of the Movies*

First edition published, November 1973

Second printing, October 1975

ISBN 0-515-03246-8

Library of Congress Catalog Card Number: 73-90437

Published by Pyramid Communications, Inc. Its trademarks, consisting of the word "Pyramid" and the portrayal of a pyramid, are registered in the United States Patent Office.
PYRAMID COMMUNICATIONS, INC.
919 Third Avenue, New York, New York 10022

(graphic design by anthony basile)

*For*
*G.L. Senior—*
*Our* Own *Cary Grant*

## ACKNOWLEDGMENTS

Audio Brandon Films, George Caudill, Homer Dickens, Kenneth G. Lawrence's Movie Memorabilia Shop of Hollywood, Leonard Maltin, Doug McClelland, Mark Ricci's Memory Shop, Romano Tozzi, and Lou Valentino.

And the companies that distributed Cary Grant's films: Columbia Pictures, Grand National Pictures, Metro-Goldwyn-Mayer Inc., Paramount Pictures Corp., RKO Radio Pictures, Twentieth Century-Fox Film Corp., United Artists Corp., Universal Pictures, and Warner Bros. Inc.

## ABOUT THE AUTHOR

Jerry Vermilye is an incurable movie addict whose reviews and articles have appeared in *Films in Review, Film Fan Monthly, Screen Facts, The Independent Film Journal,* and Andy Warhol's *InterView.* He is also the author of *Burt Lancaster;* and *Bette Davis* (Pyramid Illustrated History of the Movies). Mr. Vermilye, who lives in Manhattan, is movie-listings editor of *TV Guide.*

## ABOUT THE EDITOR

Ted Sennett is the author of *Warner Brothers Presents,* a survey of the great Warners films of the Thirties and Forties, and of *Lunatics and Lovers,* on the years of the "screwball" movie comedy. He has also written about films for magazines and newspapers. A publishing executive, he lives in New Jersey with his wife and three children.

# CONTENTS

No other male film star has been as popular for so long a period as Cary Grant. He has appeared opposite most of the top film actresses of the past forty years, with the notable exceptions of Bette Davis, Joan Crawford, and Greta Garbo—three ladies who often carried a film without a costar of comparable strength. Of his seventy-two movies, twenty-eight have opened at New York's Radio City Music Hall, the nation's most coveted showcase.

He is an actor known, not for his versatility or his ability to submerge his personality in a character, but rather for his skill at developing and maintaining the image of a handsome, well groomed man-about-town whose perfect manners, wit, and sartorial elegance are disarming. This image frequently enables him, on the screen, to throw conventions to the winds, behaving with an utter disregard for propriety—and to get away with it. And, almost without exception, he plays a character that he devised and honed to perfection: Cary Grant.

# INTRODUCTION

"When I appear on the screen," he admits, "I'm playing myself. It's harder to play yourself. I pretended to be a certain kind of man on screen, and I became that man in life. I became me. But to play yourself—your true self—is the hardest thing in the world to do. Watch people at a party. They're playing themselves like everything—but nine times out of ten the image of themselves they adopt is the wrong one. Adopt the true image of yourself, acquire a technique to project it, and the public will give you its allegiance."

Grant has long held the public's allegiance, but they prefer his familiar image in comedy. Comedy is his forte, and no one plays comedy quite like Cary Grant. Despite his personable facade, he is a very funny man. His walk—a natural tendency to bowleggedness—is funny. So are the stiff-necked turns character-

9

istic of his upper torso. And so are those ironic and distrustful expressions he effortlessly assumes toward so many of the other players in his movies. If the eyes are indeed the mirrors of the soul, then Grant's eyes—whether bemused, skeptical, steely, or shifting with apprehension—are a warning to Satan.

Seldom is Grant's hair out of place, and never is he less than heavily tanned, thus fostering a healthy-looking outward appearance that helps emphasize a devilish cleft chin and a pair of facial moles that the actor has never cared for. (They are usually airbrushed away in publicity stills.) And capping it all is that distinctive voice, with its traces of cockney.

While Cary Grant's personal life is marked by the failure of four marriages, his career has grown, prospered, and made him a multimillionaire, through a shrewd head for business and a well-known reluctance to squander his money on the trivial or unnecessary.

Grant's personal charm is the greater for his natural modesty. "I'm actually rather dull," he once said, "for all I do is relax. I was an idiot until I was forty—an actor, a bore, wrapped up in myself. Everyone tells me I've had such an interesting life, but sometimes I think it's been nothing but stomach disturbances and self-concern."

Grant is an individual, and Hollywood has never understood an individual. Hollywood never understood Cary Grant. Perhaps, this innate air of mystery helped to heighten his on-screen appeal, to keep audiences interested in his shadow-image and its reactions, even when the movie was less than excellent. Yet few of this actor's films can be classified as poor. If it is true that most actors are bad judges of what sort of roles are best for them, then Grant's record indicates that he is clearly an exception. For comedies like *Holiday*, *The Awful Truth*, *Bringing Up Baby*, and *The Philadelphia Story* belong to the richest vein of an era when Broadway and Hollywood writers were at their glittering best, whether the genre was "screwball" farce or comedy of manners. Nor was Grant strictly a *comedy* star in this vintage period of his career. Few adventure films can top *Gunga Din* in its blend of humor, action, and spectacle, and few actors can successfully bridge the gap from high comedy to pathos, as Grant did in *Penny Serenade* and *None But the Lonely Heart*, both of which won him Academy Award nominations.

The Grant finesse is partly a result of working with some of the greatest directors in Hollywood history: five films with Howard Hawks, four with Alfred Hitchcock, and three each with George Stevens, George Cukor, and Leo McCarey. "Nobody really appreciates how good an actor Cary really is," says McCarey. "I remember once he was doing a tragic scene for me. He made my hard-boiled crew bawl —and they didn't even know what the rest of the script was about!"

An important star who has worked with the actor says, "All of us are perfectionists to some extent but, believe me, it's literally a matter of life and death with Grant."

In a moment of self-appraisal, Grant once said: "The tough thing, the final thing, is to be yourself. That takes doing, and I should know. I used to be Noel Coward. Hand-plunged-in-the-pocket, y'know. It took me three long years to get my silly hand out of there, and they were three years wasted. Noel Coward is great at being Noel Coward; the role I do best is Cary Grant."

*An early portrait.*

Cary Grant began life in the first hour of Monday, the 18th of January 1904, in the southwestern seaport city of Bristol, England. He was born at home to Elias James and Elsie Kingdom Leach, middle-class Episcopalians who had lost their first son when he was only a few months old. Their second they named Archibald Alexander, or simply "Archie." In fact, "Archie Leach" remained with him through his first twenty-eight years, encompassing school, vaudeville, and even the Broadway stage. Only Hollywood would consider the name uncommercial.

A shy and introverted only child, Archie Leach had a strict and proper upbringing. His father was employed by a Bristol clothing manufacturer, a lowly position on the economic scale that prompted some conflict between Leach and his wife. If money was tight at home, young Archie was nonetheless well fed, clothed, and cared for. At four-and-a-half, he was sent to school because his mother believed him highly intelligent for his age, and convinced the local schoolmaster to accept him a year ahead of those who were his classmates.

When Archie was nine, his mother disappeared from his life under what then appeared to be

# ARCHIE LEACH- BRISTOL TO BROADWAY (1904-1930)

mysterious circumstances. He came home one day to find her gone, along with most of her personal effects. At first, he was told that she had gone away for a holiday, but the "holiday" stretched on for much too long to be true. Years passed before he learned the whole story—that Elsie Leach had suffered a nervous breakdown and had been confined to an institution. It was some twenty years before they were reunited, and undoubtedly Grant's emotional proximity to her in her later years stems from this long period of separation.

For a time, Archie's aunt, uncle, and cousins lived with them. When a change in jobs required them to move, the boy and his father moved in with the elder Mrs. Leach, his grandmother. Archie was eleven and an indifferent student. However, the following year, he managed to win a scholarship to Fairfield, a coeducational school that proved costly to the Leach family budget, due to the requirements of books, athletic equipment, and school uniforms.

Cary Grant believes his interest in a show business career began at the age of thirteen, when he first discovered the backstage workings of a professional vaudeville theater. At Fairfield, he became friends with an assistant chemistry instructor, a middle-aged man who doubled as an electrician at Bristol's Hippodrome, where he had recently established that new theater's backstage lighting system. For Archie, the Hippodrome was a magical new world, where he soon made himself useful running errands and hauling equipment in his spare time. And he got to witness, at first hand, how a vaudeville show operates. The cheerful, raucous, and resilient performers fascinated Archie. While his school curriculum failed to hold his interest, he was drawn deeper into the lights, music, and gaiety of the live theatrical performances.

At thirteen, Archie Leach was tall for his years and rather mature, and when his backstage mentor introduced him to the manager of another Bristol theater, the Empire, the apprentice electrician became even busier at the latter house—all without pay, of course. He was given the job of operating the spotlight that follows the movements of a performer from high up on a theater's beams. But a freak ac-

cident put an abrupt end to the young stagehand's budding career when a misdirected light beam exposed and thereby ruined a magician's trick-mirror act. Archie Leach retreated to the Hippodrome.

Among the more celebrated acts in England's variety theaters was the Bob Pender Troupe, consisting of teen-aged boys trained as acrobatic comics. Having determined that he wanted to break into show business, not as a professional stagehand, but rather as an entertainer, Archie Leach sought out Pender's mailing address. He then drafted a letter that would sound as though it was written by his father, signed Elias Leach's name to it, and enclosed a photograph that made him look sixteen.

Archie's bluff paid off. Pender wrote back that he wanted to meet the boy, and he enclosed train fare to Norwich, a town some three hundred miles distant. To make that long journey by himself, Archie packed a few belongings and stole away from home by night. It took courage, and he had his doubts.

In Norwich, Bob Pender and his wife liked Archie's appearance and manner, and they offered him a contract that provided for room, board, touring expenses—and ten shillings a week. In return, Archie would learn the comic turns and acrobatic stunts required of all the Pender lads. Rehearsals and exercises began at once for Archie, and for the first time he felt like a clumsy amateur. That he wasn't sent home as hopeless surprised him; that he was performing before paying customers within a week's time was nothing short of astounding to the boy. He was an actor!

It wasn't long, however, before the elder Leach located his wayward son. Inquiries at the Bristol Hippodrome revealed Archie's interest in the Bob Pender Troupe, and some amateur sleuthing soon pinpointed that act's current bookings. In Ipswich, Elias Leach reclaimed his boy—and struck up an instant rapport with Bob Pender, a fellow Mason. Oddly enough, Archie wasn't punished; he was merely brought home and sent back to Fairfield, where his daring adventure gave him an enjoyable notoriety. It also wrought permanent changes in the once-introverted Archie Leach. He was now different from his classmates. He had done something that none of the others had dared to chance, and it had made him a local celebrity.

Archie had never been an honor student. Now he proved impossible. His school pranks got him in trouble, and finally he was expelled from Fairfield under a cloud of humiliation. However, by then, Archie had reached his fourteenth birthday. His father indulgently allowed him to rejoin the Pender Troupe. If his son was to become an actor, then at least he would be well trained for it.

With Bob Pender, Archie Leach served a rigorous one-week training period in tumbling, stilt-walking, acrobatics, and dancing. Pender demanded only the best from each of his young performers, and stressed that professionalism came only through hard work and constant practice. Because the wordless Pender act depended solely on the skills of pantomime and physical ability, Archie learned some of the most valuable essentials of the acting craft, notably comic timing, economy of movement, and some choice words of wisdom: "Never stay on too long. Never let the audience get tired of you. Always leave 'em laughing and wanting more." Which is exactly what Cary Grant elected to do in 1966 at the age of sixty-two.

On tour with the Pender Troupe, Archie Leach played two shows a day. The first big thrill of his young career was returning to Bristol when the act played the Empire, and his father and friends came backstage to celebrate the occasion.

As time passed with the Pender performers, Archie became adept at comic improvisation, eventually realizing the enormous salary of a pound a week. In 1920, soon after his sixteenth birthday, he learned that Pender had signed to take the act to New York to appear in a Charles Dillingham production. But there was a catch: the contract allowed for only eight of the twelve boys then employed in the troupe. During six weeks of suspense, Archie worked hard to please his boss and be among those chosen for the trip. And his efforts paid off; they sailed on the Olympic from Southhampton that July.

Charles Dillingham, then one of Broadway's great showmen, immediately put the Pender Troupe into *Good Times*, a king-sized musical spectacle that opened in Manhattan's gigantic Hippodrome Theater on August 9, 1920. During the engagement, Pender and his boys rented a furnished apartment near the theater on noisy Eighth Avenue and, in their off-hours, experienced, first hand, the eye-opening sights and sounds of New York.

When their show finally closed, Bob Pender managed to get his boys booked for a six-month tour of the U.S., playing the Keith vaudeville circuit from Boston to Los Angeles. Their English accents helped get them dinner invitations from the socially prominent as they traveled through America's heartland, and for Archie and the other boys it was an education no amount of money could have bought. The tour closed in great style in June of 1921 at the New York Palace, the goal of all variety performers. When that engagement ended, Archie Leach informed Pender that he had decided to remain in the States, rather than return to Britain with the act.

Theatrical pickings in Manhattan have never been lucrative in midsummer, and Archie met nothing but discouragement as he made the inevitable rounds of theatrical booking offices. As an inexperienced seventeen-year-old actor, he had little to offer any legitimate play. As his savings dwindled, he moved into ever-cheaper quarters, stinted on food, and was forced to rely on the kindness of friends to keep a roof over his head. Finally, he found an offbeat job that would use one of his Pender skills—as a stilt-walking advertisement for

Tilyou's Steeplechase Park on the boardwalk in Coney Island. His pay: five dollars a day on weekdays, and twice that on weekends.

After that summer, Archie moved back to Manhattan and teamed up with a young Australian named John Kelly (long before he became Hollywood costume designer "Orry-Kelly"), who made and sold hand-painted neckties as a start of a designing career that would (thirty years later) win him an Academy Award for *An American in Paris*. Archie peddled the ties and even helped make them. But he never lost sight of his theatrical dreams, and eventually he organized his own vaudeville act patterned after the Pender Troupe, but sometimes incorporating dialogue skits. By 1923, he had gained enough experience touring the lesser vaudeville circuits to attract big-time talent scouts. But internal dissent broke up the act, and Archie went his own way, accepting nightclub engagements and one-night stands to keep himself solvent. He gained invaluable experience as a "straight man" for comedians, developing the immaculate timing that would become Cary Grant's trademark. When his big break came in 1927, he was ready.

At twenty-three, Archie Leach agreed to play a benefit one September night, working with a comedian who arrived too drunk to perform. Left to fend for himself, Archie managed to improvise an alternate program. In the time allotted him, he did some acrobatic dancing, told jokes and sang a few songs. The next day an associate of producer Arthur Hammerstein contacted Archie to laud his performance and offer him a featured role in an Otto Harbach-Oscar Hammerstein II operetta called *Golden Dawn* with Louise Hunter and Paul Gregory. Archie played an Anzac (Australian) prisoner of war and was the secondary romantic interest. The show opened on November 30, 1927 at Hammerstein's Theatre, and garnered Archie Leach several brief notices of the "handsome young newcomer" variety. *Golden Dawn* failed to achieve the stature of a hit but ran until spring, tallying up a respectable run of 184 performances.°

Arthur Hammerstein, producer of *Golden Dawn*, was sufficiently impressed with Archie's work to cast him in *Polly*, a song

---

°*Golden Dawn* was filmed by Warner Bros. in 1930 in primitive color. The stars were Vivienne Segal and Walter Woolf King.

and dance version of David Belasco's 1917 Ina Claire vehicle, *Polly With a Past*. But songs didn't help *Polly*; it closed in two weeks. For Archie, however, unemployment was gradual: his contract guaranteed him full salary for six weeks. This factor proved a frustrating handicap when his Hammerstein contract prevented his accepting an offer from the latter's archenemy, Florenz Ziegfeld, who wanted Archie as a replacement for his male star Jack Donahue in the hit musical *Rosalie*.

Soon afterwards, Hammerstein sold Archie Leach's contract to the Shubert theatrical empire, and in late January of 1929, Archie opened in the Shubert's production of *Boom Boom*, a musical comedy starring Jeanette MacDonald. Archie had had enough foresight to negotiate a run-of-the-show contract that guaranteed him $450 a week. The critics liked the young Englishman's performance, and *Boom Boom* enjoyed a run of seventy-two performances. That summer, he and Jeanette MacDonald both tested for motion pictures at Paramount's Astoria studios in Queens. Miss MacDonald went on to Hollywood and *The Love Parade*, opposite Maurice Chevalier. Archie Leach not only failed to make a favorable impression, but was told that a thick neck and bowlegs had handicapped his success.

That autumn, the Shubert brothers cast Archie in an altered version of Johann Strauss's perennial hit operetta, *Die Fledermaus*, now retitled *A Wonderful Night*. Opposite Gladys Baxter and Mary McCoy, Archie had the male lead and was very well received by the press. The show ran for 125 performances. He took the male lead opposite Queenie Smith in a road company of her hit musical, *Street Singer*. The tour lasted well into the spring of 1931, and Archie then signed to play leads in a repertory season of musicals with the famed St. Louis Municipal Opera. That summer, singing his way from *Rio Rita* and *Rose Marie* to *Irene* and *Countess Maritza*, he became a great local favorite and inspired *Variety*'s Midwest correspondent to write about him at some length. This led to his being signed for the Broadway production of *Nikki*, a musical written by John Monk Saunders as a vehicle for his actress wife, Fay Wray. *Nikki* lasted for only thirty-nine performances, but it gave Archie Leach the idea to change his name. In the cast of *Nikki*, he played the role of Cary Lockwood.

During 1931, Archie Leach made a film debut so inauspicious that, to date, no film reference has taken note of it. In Paramount's Astoria studios, he played a non-singing supporting role in a ten-minute musical short called *Singapore Sue*, released the following year as a Paramount program filler. The stars of the movie were Anna Chang and Joe Wong, with Millard Mitchell and Archie as sailors in an Oriental café setting. Casey Robinson, later known for his screenplays of such films as *Dark Victory* and *Kings Row*, wrote and directed the featurette. It wasn't released until the following year, after Archie had become Cary Grant.

Archie Leach's burgeoning Broadway career held every promise of building and continuing, but he had other ideas in mind, mainly a career in Hollywood. Quite a few of his New York theatrical acquaintances had left New York for the far more lucrative West Coast movie studios. Seasoned stage performers had a distinct advantage over the average attractive, or even talented, young actor flocking to the film capital in search of success. Archie Leach believed he was prepared for success in movies—if he went after it.

A Broadway crony recom-

# CARY GRANT - THE EARLY YEARS AT PARAMOUNT (1931-1935)

mended that Archie look up a director named Marion Gering when he reached Hollywood. Gering arranged for the young man to assist an actress being considered for a Paramount contract by playing opposite her in a screen test he was slated to direct. This time the circumstances were more fortuitous than during the ill-fated Astoria test. A complete scene was memorized, rehearsed, and played, and two hours of rehearsal were allowed with Gering before the actual shooting. The scene ran six minutes, and won Archie a contract with Paramount Pictures. His female partner failed to impress anyone, and was forgotten.

The studio had signed Archie Leach at a starting salary of $450 a week, but they didn't like his name. Paramount ordered him to find a new one. His friend, Fay Wray, suggested he use his *Nikki* name, Cary Lockwood. He liked "Cary," but for some reason, the "Lockwood" portion displeased him. The moguls at Paramount provided a solution: according to the actor,

*SINGAPORE SUE (1932). With Anna Chang.*

"They went down this long list of names and came up with 'Grant': I said it was fine and asked them how much they'd pay me to take it." But the starting salary remained fixed at $450. And so, at twenty-eight, Archie Leach left behind a mainly musical stage career for a largely tuneless film career—as Cary Grant.

In the early thirties, the Hollywood studios obtained considerable "mileage" from their contract players. During 1932, the year of Cary's movie bow, he was seen in no less than seven feature films—as well as the brief *Singapore Sue*. His roles varied in size and importance, but they provided him with the exposure to the public that, in those long-past days of Hollywood's star system, could make or break a career.

His first full-length movie was an adaptation of Avery Hopwood's 1925 stage farce, *Naughty Cinderella*. Paramount re-titled it *This Is the Night*. In that film, the decidedly British Mr. Grant was cast as an Olym-

*THIS IS THE NIGHT (1932). With Lily Damita.*

*THIS IS THE NIGHT (1932). With Thelma Todd, Roland Young and Charles Ruggles.*

*SINNERS IN THE SUN (1932). With Carole Lombard.*

pic javelin thrower with the un-Anglican name of Stepan Mendanich. Against sets representing Venice and Paris, Thelma Todd portrayed his wife, a flashy blonde who attracts the attentions of playboy-philanderer Roland Young. In the course of the subsequent marital mix-ups, Grant becomes attracted to Lily Damita, who is posing as the wife of Young. In this comedy with music, Grant was billed fourth under the two ladies, Young, and Charles Ruggles. The movie was handsomely produced, and Frank Tuttle's direction helped the newcomer to win such critical approbation as *The New York Times*' "Cary Grant is

efficient as the stalwart Stepan" and the *New York Herald-Tribune*'s "In an undistinguished straight role, Cary Grant plays with amiable assurance."

In the trivial Carole Lombard vehicle, *Sinners in the Sun*, routinely directed by Alexander Hall, Grant turned up eighth in the cast as a ne'er-do-well playboy named Ridgeway who, briefly, was one of the men in the busy social life of clothes-model Doris Blake (Lombard). In the standard Depression plot, Lombard played a restless working girl who leaves her garage-mechanic beau (Chester Morris) to carouse with the Long Island social set, only to learn that love is more important than money and affairs. Based on a story called *The Beachcomber* by novelist Mildred Cram, this superficial drama was distinguished only by the style and glamour that Lombard brought to it. *Variety* called it "a very weak picture with an unimpressive future before it." In his few scenes, Cary Grant was barely noticed.

Grant had even less to do in *Merrily We Go to Hell*, a comedy-drama with a meandering script about the seesaw marriage of a chic heiress (Sylvia Sidney in a change of pace from her customary drab roles) and an alcohol-prone reporter-turned-playwright (Fredric March). Under Dorothy Arzner's direc-tion, the two stars gave Edwin Justus Mayer's lackluster screenplay more charm and vitality than it merited. Cary Grant's abbreviated appearance occurred in theatre sequences, in which he played the leading man in March's play—an actor named Charles Exeter.

His next film, *Devil and the Deep* was a sex melodrama tailored for Charles Laughton, Tallulah Bankhead, and Gary Cooper, and the first of three films Cary Grant would make under the direction of the man responsible for his Paramount contract, Marion Gering. As Lieutenant Jaeckel, Grant appeared only in the picture's first half hour, serving to establish the destructive

*MERRILY WE GO TO HELL (1932). With Sylvia Sidney and Fredric March.*

*DEVIL AND THE DEEP (1932). With Charles Laughton.*

relationship between the faithless Pauline Sturm (Bankhead) and her insanely jealous husband (Laughton), commander of the submarine on which Jaeckel is stationed. Because Sturm rightfully suspects an affair between Pauline and Jaeckel, he has him transferred elsewhere—only to meet with more formidable competition in Lieutenant Sempter (Cooper). This high-voltage trio contributes richly to the film's lurid plot, which ends with the drowning of Sturm in a claustrophobic underwater climax. In a ripe display of histrionics, the portly Laughton steals *Devil and the Deep* from his more glamorous co-stars.

*Blonde Venus* is probably the least of the seven exotic melodramas made by the extraordinary director-star team of Josef von Sternberg and Marlene Dietrich. If its bizarre and rambling plot seems improvised, the director has admitted that he whipped the story together as an alternative to the scripts Paramount then wanted him to film with Dietrich. As Helen Faraday, the German star is seldom off-camera, suffused in glowing, soft-focus photography by Bert Glennon, and suffering exquisitely through the kaleidoscopic role requirements of cafe entertainer, loving wife, noble, self-sacrificing mother, and reluctant prostitute.

The preposterous *Stella Dallas* script has her go through hell to obtain large sums required to provide treatment for her husband Edward (Herbert Marshall), a victim of radium poisoning. To do so, she becomes the mistress of Nick Townsend (Grant), a wealthy playboy who sets her up in a luxurious apartment of her own. When Edward learns the truth, Helen flees with her child and meets hard times. Later, she goes back to singing in clubs and becomes the toast of Paris, with Townsend again her most frequent escort. Eventually, Helen confesses everything to her husband, and they are reconciled.

In this film, his fifth for 1932, Cary Grant's charm, looks, and romantic style made a considerable impression on Depression-era audiences. Critical reaction to *Blonde Venus* was far from kind, but Mordaunt Hall in *The New York Times* thought Grant "worthy of a much better role." Paramount executives liked the young actor's work, too, and there was talk of a remake of Valentino's 1922 hit, *Blood and Sand*, with either Dietrich or Bankhead as the siren who destroys him. He was also considered a potential replacement for one of that studio's less cooperative stars, Gary Cooper, and was assigned roles in *Hot Saturday* and *Madame Butterfly* that the lanky actor had turned down.

In *Hot Saturday*, Cary Grant received top billing for the first time, costarring with Nancy Carroll, once one of Paramount's leading stars, but now sadly waning. Clearly, the studio heads deemed their handsome new actor destined for a brighter future than Miss Carroll, though *Hot Saturday* is strictly her story. Under William A. Seiter's direction, she plays Ruth Brock, a small-town bank clerk who is believed by the local gossips to have been compromised by Romer Sheffield (Grant), a notorious playboy whose chauffered car brings her home at a scandalously late hour from a party at his lakeside home. The girl's innocence is eventually proven but, at the party announcing her engagement to Bill Fadden (Randolph Scott), her childhood sweetheart, the scandal reaches *his* ears. When her angered fiancé breaks off with her, Ruth retaliates by boldly running to Romer and spending the night with him. The next day, she returns to inform Bill and her family that she is now *truly* guilty of the misconduct they had once all too easily believed. At the fadeout, Ruth and Romer are driving to New York

*BLONDE VENUS (1932). With Marlene Dietrich.*

*HOT SATURDAY (1932). With Nancy Carroll.*

and, presumably, a minister. In *Hot Saturday*'s altered remake, the 1941 Deanna Durbin vehicle, *Nice Girl?*, the young lady ends with the boy-next-door (Robert Stack), over her more sophisticated swain (Franchot Tone, in the Grant role).

In his first nominal lead, Grant was rather wooden, particularly in contrast to the over-exuberant playing of Nancy Carroll at her most Clara Bow-like. As the small-town rake, he is appropriately sophisticated and convincingly smooth with the ladies —Ruth tells him, "You're considered too dangerous for local consumption"—and he is an unquestionably natty dresser,

whether in white suit, fedora and two-tone shoes, or Japanese samurai dressing gown. But the script allows him no opportunity for the obligatory character transition.

It is interesting to note how un-camerawise Grant was in 1932. He often allows a fellow player to enjoy the full benefit of the lens, while showing the audience the *under*-side of his upturned jaw or a three-quarters *rear* profile of his face. But it wasn't long before he would learn the full value of light and camera placement in relation to the actor. During the making of *Hot Saturday*, Cary Grant and Randolph Scott became fast friends. At the former's suggestion, they took a house together —the better to save money. Grant's celebrated penchant for thrift later came in for some sharp comment from their mutual friend, Carole Lombard: "Cary opened the bills, Randy wrote the checks, and if Cary could talk someone out of a stamp, he mailed them."

*Madame Butterfly*, Cary Grant's seventh and last 1932 film, was little help in his career. As in David Belasco's play, the inspiration for Giacomo Puccini's durable opera, the plot's main focus is on its heroine, Cho-Cho-San (Sylvia Sidney), the sweet little geisha beauty who marries selfish Lieutenant Pinkerton (Grant), a U.S. Navy man temporarily stationed in Yokohama. Eventually, he must return home, promising to come back "when the robins build their nests." By the time he returns— several years later—"Butterfly" has his son, unknown to Pinkerton. She has lived only for his re-

*MADAME BUTTERFLY (1932). With Sylvia Sidney.*

turn, and when she discovers that he now has an American wife (bland Sheila Terry) and considers their union no more than a passing romance—a pleasant memory—Cho-Cho-San decides to "die with honor, rather than live without it."

Miss Sidney is lovely and appealing as the tragic heroine and, almost single-handedly, maintains the viewer's attention, since Marion Gering directs the picture at a pace too sluggish for the creaky plot. Without the sumptuous Puccini score, which the studio uneasily blended in the background with its own "incidental" music, the hoary old tearjerker holds little interest. As the caddish Pinkerton, Grant is given little to do. In the opera, the character at least has the rousing tenor-baritone duet "Dovunque al mondo" and his long, idyllic duet with Butterfly that closes act 1, as well as the plaintive act 3 aria "Addio, fiorito asil." By way of compensation, the 1932 film has ex-Broadway tenor Grant sing to Sylvia Sidney a little ditty entitled "My Flower of Japan," neatly turned out for the occasion by W. Franke Harling and Ralph Rainger. Undoubtedly, it was easier for him to *sing* to Sylvia than to stand by while she called him "Honorable Lieutenant, the most best nice man in all the world."

If *Madame Butterfly* did little to enhance Grant's burgeoning career, neither did it harm him, for women could hardly fail to notice Cary Grant's dark and handsome good looks, enhanced by his naval uniforms. The actor's striking physical appearance was exactly what now gave an added boost to his film future, in the buxom form of an unexpected benefactress—Mae West.

According to West, Grant was an *extra* when she chose him as her leading man for her second motion picture, *She Done Him Wrong*, released early in 1933. Quite obviously, Mae's own memory (or her knowledge of Hollywood history) does *her* wrong! At any rate, Cary Grant supposedly first caught the sex queen's eye on the Paramount lot, where she asked his name of a studio official. According to reports, the man replied: "Oh, that's Cary Grant. He's making *Butterfly* right now with Sylvia Sidney." To which West is said to have quipped, "I don't care if he's making Little Nell. If he can talk, I'll take him."

The controversial Miss West was, at that time, setting Hollywood on its collective ear. A much-censored Broadway playwright and star, due to the carnal frankness of her handcrafted starring vehicles like *Sex* and *The Pleasure Man*, Mae, in a few brief scenes, had easily walked off with the 1932 *Night After Night*. In the words of its star, George Raft, "In this picture, Mae West stole everything but the cameras."

Based on her classic, often-revived stage hit *Diamond Lil*, *She Done Him Wrong* is also the most durable of Mae's movies. Set in Manhattan's brawling Bowery during the 1890s, it centers on a celebrated belle named Lou (in the play, of course, it was "Lil"), a saloon entertainer who collects men and diamonds. The Hays Office demanded changes, and the film

went into production late in 1932 under the title *Ruby Red*. Mae supervised the Harvey Thew-John Bright screen adaptation and managed to obtain an unusual consideration from Paramount: a week's rehearsals for the leading cast members prior to shooting. Actual filming was accomplished in a near-record eighteen days.

For 1933, the movie's plot is simple and salacious enough to cause a censor sleepless nights. Lou ("I'm one of the finest women who ever walked the streets") is the mistress of Gus Jordan (Noah Beery Sr.), who operates a Bowery dance hall, when he's not running a white-slave ring or counterfeiting on

*SHE DONE HIM WRONG (1933). With Mae West.*

*SHE DONE HIM WRONG (1933). With Mae West.*

the side. Lou becomes single-mindedly attracted to Captain Cummings (Grant), the Salvation Army man from next door, and unintentionally helps him break up the white-slave racket, before discovering that he's really a federal agent.

Grant's occasional scenes as straight man to Mae West produce chemical sparks and a few memorable lines. After appealing to her to help quiet the saloon's nightly racket, he politely adds, "I'm sorry to be taking your time." To which Mae rejoinders, "What do you think my time is for?" On another occasion, just before an exit, Mae pauses, gives him the once-over and murmurs, "You can be had." Perhaps most famous (and misquoted) of all is her Grant-directed offer: "Why don't you come up sometime and see me?" Then, as he hesitates: "Come on up. I'll tell your fortune."

In the end, Lady Lou goes off in the personal custody of Captain Cummings, bearing a new diamond ring and seated in his private car. "You bad girl," he quips, a twinkle in his eye. "You'll find out," retorts Lou.

Whatever seemed acceptable in the original screenplay became soaked in innuendo by the time Mae West had finished with it. The film's director, Lowell Sherman, wisely let her have her way, with the result that *She Done Him Wrong* became a comedy sensation and a box-office record-breaker. Six months after its release, this movie was cited as a prime argument for establishing the National Legion of Decency—and the impetus for a major censorship crackdown on the U.S. motion picture industry.

Cary Grant later spoke of his association with Miss West: "I learned everything from her. Well, not everything but almost everything. She knows so much. Her instinct is so true, her timing so perfect, her grasp of the situation so right."

*She Done Him Wrong* proved a definite step forward for Grant; his next film did not. In *The Woman Accused,* he again appeared opposite vivacious Nancy Carroll, this time in a shipboard-murder melodrama in which the heroine, Glenda O'Brien, accidentally kills her ex-lover (Louis Calhern) when he threatens a life of happiness with Jeffrey Baxter (Grant), her lawyer-fiancé. In the end, Jeffrey helps get Glenda acquitted, and the case is dismissed. Screen-

*THE WOMAN ACCUSED (1933). With Nancy Carroll.*

*THE EAGLE AND THE HAWK (1933). As Henry Crocker.*

*THE EAGLE AND THE HAWK (1933). With Fredric March.*

writer Bayard Veiller was hard put to make something of what had originally been a *Liberty* magazine serial with an unusual gimmick: ten well-known novelists, among them Zane Grey, Vicki Baum, and Viña Delmar, had each written a separate chapter of the story. Paul Sloane, whose career never rose above the "programmer" level, directed this banal mixture, none too evenly.

Of greater interest is the actor's work in *The Eagle and the Hawk,* Stuart Walker's strong film about the Royal Flying Corps in World War I. Among the best of Grant's early movies, this John Monk Saunders story

cast him opposite Fredric March in an antiwar tale of bitter enemies who, nevertheless, form an efficient flying team. In the end, Grant, a callous aerial gunner who takes pleasure in killing the enemy, turns noble. After March, his alcoholic commanding officer, commits suicide during an emotional crack-up, Grant secretly takes the body up in his plane, riddles it with bullets, and deliberately crashes to the ground, to imply a hero's death. Aside from a gratuitous romantic interlude involving March and Carole Lombard for marquee value, it was a vigorous male-adventure yarn, capably directed by Walker, who wisely con-

*GAMBLING SHIP (1933). With Benita Hume.*

cerned himself more with the development of character than with the action sequences. For the most part, *The Eagle and the Hawk*'s aerial footage was taken from such past war-in-the-air epics as *The Dawn Patrol, Lilac Time,* and the classic *Wings.*

*Gambling Ship,* Gary Grant's fourth 1933 film, is a familiar but entertaining action story about mobsters operating off the California coast. Grant plays Ace Corbin, a gangster already retired from crime, despite his youthful appearance. He falls for a mystery woman, Eleanor La Velle (Benita Hume, the wife of Ronald Colman), who happens to be the mistress of a gambling-ship owner (Arthur Vinton). The Max Marcin-Seton I. Miller screenplay hinges on the fact that neither Ace nor Eleanor knows of the other's past. Undoubtedly, *Gambling Ship* is no worse—and probably somewhat better—than many a "programmer" that the 1930s Paramount contract player was obliged to appear in enroute to better things. *Variety*'s critic thought that the film reinforced Grant's potential as a major box-office draw for the ladies.

Cary Grant is the only star of his caliber who has enjoyed two major film appearances opposite Mae West. Before 1933 was over, he was again her leading man, this time in the rowdy comedy *I'm No Angel.* Quite possibly, it is the most entertaining of all her films. As usual, the Westian innuendos provided the comic strength of this story about the social progress of a midway carnival dancer and lion tamer named Tira (pronounced "Tyra") who goes through a succession of smitten males as she rises to millionaire's gal. Grant played Jack Clayton, a rich but elusive playboy and Mae's true love, whom she nevertheless sues for a million dollars, charging him with breach of promise. Serving as her own counsel, Tira wins her case by personally cross-examining her man (in a hilarious scene) —and winning him, as well.

Mae, of course, was responsible for the leering script, a cleverly contrived bundle of wisecracks, good-natured sex, and snatches of suggestive songs, which she sang herself.

*I'm No Angel* was directed by Wesley Ruggles, who had learned the craft of comedy as a Keystone Kop in the early 1900s and would later be responsible for some of the more inspired comedy scenes of Claudette Colbert (*The Gilded Lily*), Carole Lombard (*True Confession*), and Jean Arthur (*Too Many Husbands*).

At the box office, *I'm No Angel* outgrossed even *She Done*

I'M NO ANGEL (1933). With Mae West.

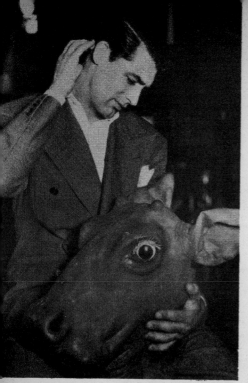

**ALICE IN WONDERLAND (1933).**
Contemplating his Mock Turtle costume.

Again, Cary Grant served as a suave and handsome foil to the vulgarly funny West, whose inspired screenplay contributed to the language such catchphrases as "Beulah, peel me a grape," and "When I'm good, I'm very good. But when I'm bad, I'm better." Fortunately, *I'm No Angel* escaped unscathed as the newly-formed Motion Picture Production Code instituted rigid rules about displays, or intimations, of sexual matters.

Before the close of 1933, Cary Grant appeared as himself, along with countless other film celebrities, in ten-minute Paramount shorts entitled *Hollywood on Parade*, followed by a star-studded version of the Lewis Carroll classic *Alice in Wonderland*, released for Christmas. As the mournful Mock Turtle, who sang tearfully about "beautiful, beautiful soup," Grant was heavily disguised. In the capable hands of art director William Cameron Menzies (*Things To Come*), the storybook fantasy came enchantingly to life, aided by the inventive direction of Norman Z. McLeod, then a recent veteran of Marx Brothers madness (*Horse Feathers, Monkey Business*) and the omnibus comedy-drama *If I Had a Million*. To play Alice, Paramount had imported young Ida Lupino

*Him Wrong*, and became one of the great comedy hits of the 1930s. In its review, *Variety* noted, "Mae West is today the biggest conversation-provoker, free-space grabber and all-around boxoffice bet in the country," concluding with "She's as hot an issue as Hitler." Indeed, Mae and her two 1933 blockbusters have been credited with saving Paramount at a time when that studio was seriously considering selling out to Metro-Goldwyn-Mayer.

*THIRTY-DAY PRINCESS (1934). With Sylvia Sidney.*

from England, but found her much too sophisticated for the role. Instead, they gave the part to Charlotte Henry, a diminutive teenager who had played in several Fox and Tiffany features.

(She was to fade away several years later via Monogram and Republic.) The critics generally liked Miss Henry, and they particularly singled out Grant's Mock Turtle, W.C. Fields'

Humpty Dumpty, Alison Skipworth's Duchess, and Charles Ruggles' March Hare. Working mainly from Carroll's *Alice's Adventures in Wonderland*, with borrowed helpings from its sequel *Alice Through the Looking-Glass*, screenwriter Joseph L. Mankiewicz (thirteen years before his directorial debut with *Dragonwyck*) prepared a unique cut-by-cut script, which Menzies had illustrated profusely. Many consider this the best version of *Alice in Wonderland* yet filmed.

Despite his busy professional life, Grant somehow found time for romance in 1933. In his studio's commissary, friends had introduced the actor to Virginia Cherrill, a blonde English divorcée who is best remembered as the blind waif in Chaplin's 1931 silent film, *City Lights*. She had just completed *The Nuisance* with Lee Tracy and Madge Evans at MGM and was under contract to Fox. Virginia and Grant began seeing each other for lunch and dinner dates, parties and movie premieres. On February 9, 1934, they were married in London. The union was short-lived. Early that summer rumors began circulating about marital problems, and by mid-September it was known that Virginia had moved out of their home. On the fifth of October, Los Angeles newspapers ran front-page reports that Grant had been rushed to the hospital unconscious, and that "poison tablets" had been found by his bedside. He later claimed that he had merely been drunk, a normal reaction to his marital woes. Their divorce became final the following March. With her Hollywood career having dwindled to leads in minor films, Virginia Cherrill returned to England and wed the Earl of Jersey. Cary Grant resumed Santa Monica housekeeping arrangements with his pal Randolph Scott.

In 1934, Grant had another busy year, costarring in four comedies for Paramount and playing opposite Loretta Young on loan-out to another studio. *Thirty-Day Princess* reunited him with Sylvia Sidney in a slight but entertaining fairy tale about an actress hired to impersonate visiting royalty. She had a dual role, including a polite confrontation scene in which actress Sidney chats with princess Sidney (mouthing a curious Cho-Cho-San accent, despite having come from the mythical Mittel European kingdom of Taronia.) Grant was Porter Madison III, the young newspaper publisher who first opposes granting the princess a large loan for her impoverished country, but changes his mind as he falls in love with her. The Preston Sturges-Frank Partos screenplay was adapted from a novel by the prolific Clarence Budington Kelland, and Marion Gering's direction, with its occasional Lubitsch-like touches, indicated a somewhat more comfortable fusion of talents than *Madame Butterfly*, his previous encounter with the same stars.

By this time, Grant had grown sufficiently camerawise to avoid the bad lighting and camera angles that had once detracted from his love scenes. Smoothly self-assured and always immaculately attired, he now displayed a penchant for hands-in-pockets that nevertheless failed to destroy the sharp tailoring of his array of double-breasted suits. Perhaps the pocket gestures were a directorial solution for Cary's ever-busier hand gestures. In *Thirty-Day Princess*, the Grant arms and hands are at their busiest.

For *Born to Be Bad*, Cary Grant was loaned to producer Darryl Zanuck, whose 20th Century Pictures (before merging with Fox) were then being released through United Artists. Actor-director Lowell Sherman could do little with a melodramatic soap-opera-like script by actor Ralph Graves. The movie was not a financial success, and its only point of interest is the untypical casting of the sweet

*BORN TO BE BAD (1934). With Henry Travers, Loretta Young and Howard Lang.*

Loretta Young as a tough unwed mother (appropriately named Lettie Strong) trying to reclaim her son from the wealthy family that adopted him. Grant played Malcolm Trevor, the married but childless trucking executive who fights to keep his adopted son, despite the calculating Lettie's efforts to seduce and blackmail him. Reportedly, there was trouble with the Hays Office, and part of the story had to be re-filmed—which might account for an unconvincing ending in which Lettie repents her actions.

Back at Paramount, Grant was involved in the farcical plot machinations of *Kiss and Make-Up* and *Ladies Should Listen*, both released during the summer of 1934.

*Kiss and Make-Up* was directed by Broadway veteran Harlan Thompson. Originally entitled *Cosmetic*, this Stephen Bekeffi script, once rejected by Sylvia Sidney, is a decidedly odd, offbeat—but curiously amusing little comedy. Almost a musical (its cast members are required to burst into unexpected song at whimsical turns of the plot), *Kiss and Make-Up* has a pleasant Leo Robin-Ralph Rainger score from which one number—"Love Divided by Two," which the team wrote expressly for Cary to sing —became a modest hit on its own. The plot is frivolous and gay (in both senses of the word), with both Grant and Edward Everett Horton affecting a farce style that can only be called "high camp," by today's standards. Cary plays Dr. Maurice Lamar, owner and operator of an unusual Paris beauty emporium at which he miraculously remodels plain and unlovely females into creatures of exceptional grace and beauty. When the dashing doctor falls in love with his most expert Pygmalion job, Eve (Genevieve Tobin), he marries the lady, only to discover that she has no time to be a wife; her vain beauty-upkeep consumes her time and her interest. By the fade-out, having wrecked his salon, Lamar winds up with his secretary, Anne (Helen Mack), a plain but attractive girl who's been after him all along. "It succeeds to a remarkable degree in being dull," said *The New York Times*.

An equally frivolous French farce is *Ladies Should Listen*, an argument in defense of eavesdropping, in which Julian de Lussac (Grant), an eligible bachelor and successful businessman, is saved from ruin by an enterprising and smitten hotel telephone girl (Frances Drake). The idea was fairly amusing, but the dialogue held little sparkle and

*KISS AND MAKE-UP (1934). With Genevieve Tobin.*

the efforts of Cary Grant and Edward Everett Horton to keep the bubble from bursting only seem strained. Frank Tuttle, who had just directed Eddie Cantor's *Roman Scandals,* could offer little assistance. An interesting footnote: Ann (then known as "Clara Lou") Sheridan, later one of Grant's happiest costars (*I Was a Male War Bride*) played bits in both *Kiss and Make-Up* and *Ladies Should Listen.* In the former, she and Jacqueline Wells (later Julie Bishop) are beauty shop assistants; in the latter, Ann is a switchboard girl.

Paramount next cast him opposite the free-lancing Elissa Landi in a mixture of farce and opera called *Enter Madame.* The previous year, Landi had played the sweet Christian heroine of Cecil B. DeMille's *The Sign of the Cross* at Paramount. *Enter Madame* offered the actress a challenging change of pace as a temperamental opera diva named Lisa della Robbia; it offered Grant yet another chance to play well-dressed second fiddle to a female costar. Though miming her way through operatic scenes from *Tosca* and *Cavalleria Rusticana* (the voice belonged to Nina Koshetz), Landi displayed a charming Italian accent and an expert flair for farce. Overshadowed, Grant was attractive but callow, in this love-versus-career story about a husband who rebels against running second to his wife's career. For comfort, he takes up with another woman (Sharon Lynn), but ends with his wife, when they decide to try again.

*The New York Times* called *Enter Madame*, "just a farce with music." Seen today, it is a slight, rather sluggish romantic comedy that bogs down in trivial plot complications. On the plus side, Elissa Landi is delightful, and both she and Cary Grant are beautifully photographed, whether in lingering close-up or sartorially perfect long-shot. But Grant appears to be merely biding his time amid the Art Deco settings.

Finally, in *Wings in the Dark* (1935), Cary Grant had a welcome change of pace—as a blinded flier in this peacetime aviation drama. Myrna Loy, borrowed from MGM for the oc-

casion and awarded top billing, played a daring stunt pilot. The contrived romantic plot had Ken Gordon (Grant), his sight lost in a stove accident, invent a device for flying blind—that luckily comes in handy when, returning from a solo flight from Moscow, Sheila Mason (Loy) loses her bearings in the fog over Long Island. In the incredibly melodramatic climax, blind Ken steals a plane and goes up to help Sheila. Then, having rescued the lady (who's also his fiancée) he decides on a noble death for himself, to avoid being a burden to her. But Sheila saves him by smashing her plane into his as they come in for a landing, thus causing a small miracle: Ken's shocked into regaining his vision! So, despite all sense or reason, the film has a happy ending.

So much of *Wings in the*

*LADIES SHOULD LISTEN (1934). With Frances Drake.*

*ENTER MADAME (1935). With Elissa Landi, Cecelia Parker and Frank Albertson.*

**WINGS IN THE DARK (1935). With Myrna Loy.**

*Dark* is visually exciting (fine aerial and stunt photography) and dramatically valid under James Flood's direction, it is a pity that the screenplay by Jack Kirkland and Frank Partos gets out of hand. In their first appearance together, Grant and Loy make a good team. In fact, he very credibly delineates the inward, as well as the outward, manifestations of blindness—a distinct change from the usual Cary Grant image of suave, bantering playboy. He is particularly effective in one sequence requiring a difficult character transition. Embittered by the accident that appears to have ended his career, Ken sits glumly in the country house to which he has retreated. His friend Nick (Hobart Cavanaugh) brings him a Seeing Eye dog, which he angrily rejects. But Nick leaves the animal behind. Grant's subsequent scene with the dog, ranges movingly from dislike to affectionate gratitude when he falls over a piece of furniture and realizes, and responds to, his need for a creature whose love isn't based on pity.

Paramount had done so well with their Gary Cooper film *The Lives of a Bengal Lancer* that they now followed it with *The Last Outpost*, a rather ordinary romantic melodrama that bore a resemblance to its predecessor mainly through a similarity of backgrounds—British warfare on the Indian frontier. Where the Cooper film focused on he-man adventure, rousing charges and skirmishes, to the complete exclusion of love interest, *The Last Outpost* aimed for the best of both genres: the first half was devoted to red-blooded action and heroics—and the second part, to a triangular romance hauled in to interest the distaff trade.

Sporting a dashing moustache in the Douglas Fairbanks tradition, Grant played Captain Michael Andrews, wounded in Kurdistan but saved from death by John Stevenson (Claude Rains), a member of British Intelligence. Recovering his health in Cairo, Andrews is nursed back to health by Rosemary Haydon (Gertrude Michael), who just happens to be the wife of Stevenson. Naturally, they fall in love, with much jealousy and soul-searching consuming valuable footage. In the finale, back in the Sahara, the revenge-minded Stevenson suffers a change of heart and, instead, gives his life to save his wife's lover.

The script, a collaboration of Charles Brackett, Frank Partos, and Philip MacDonald, suffers from confused intentions.

*THE LAST OUTPOST (1935). As Michael Andrews.*

Although Rains took the acting honors, Grant managed to make something quite likable of a superficial and none-too-cerebral character. And, as if to accentuate its split-level story, *The Last Outpost* represents a team effort by directors Louis Gasnier and Charles Barton, both veterans of low-budget movies.

By 1935, Cary Grant's willingness to continue at Paramount in the tall shadow of Gary Cooper had dwindled considerably.

*THE LAST OUTPOST (1935). With Gertrude Michael.*

No longer was Grant a motion picture novice in need of cinematic exposure. Yet, it seemed, his career might continue as a never-ending succession of Cooper rejections and hand-me-downs. He was champing at the bit, beginning to kick up his own heels. At that time, his studio decided to loan him out to RKO—not for a leading part, but in *support* of that studio's reigning dramatic star, Katharine Hepburn. Paramount thought they had relegated Cary Grant to the dunce corner; instead, they had paved the way for a milestone in the actor's career.

One film he never got to appear in was Henry Hathaway's *Spawn of the North*, for which location footage was shot in Alaska during late 1936 and early 1937. Grant was slated to costar with Carole Lombard and Randolph Scott, but Lombard contracted influenza, delaying studio production. Eventually, the film was made with an entirely new cast, headed by Henry Fonda, George Raft, and Dorothy Lamour.

Cary Grant's RKO film, *Sylvia Scarlett*, is among his most important motion pictures. Not only is it the first of four notable collaborations with Katharine Hepburn, but it is also the first time Grant worked under a really top-notch director—George Cukor. In addition, the role offered him the sort of change of pace no one at Paramount had seen fit to give him, for cockney con man Jimmy Monkley is distinctly a *character* part. Gone are the well-tailored suits, the suave elegance, and the fine manners. Instead, we see a raffish lout of lower-class English speech patterns, none too pleasant a person —but far more interesting than any screen character the actor had previously attempted.

Adapted from Compton Mackenzie's 1918 novel, *The Early Life and Adventures of Sylvia Scarlett*, the movie related a strange, picaresque, almost allegorical tale of vagabond thieves who take to the road as touring actors. In one delightful scene, dressed in Pierrot costumes, the ensemble (Grant, Hepburn, Edmund Gwenn, and Dennie Moore) burst into an infectious cabaret version of "By the Beautiful Sea."

The mystified critics, while praising Hepburn's performance, deplored the fact that she spent

## CUKOR TURNS THE TIDE - SOUR GRAPES AND A VINTAGE HARVEST

most of the film disguised as a boy. George Cukor has readily admitted that *Sylvia Scarlett* was ahead of its time in 1936, when its poetic twists of dialogue, its unexpected turns of plot, and its Sir James M. Barrie-like innocence and whimsy angered and confused the press and public.

Despite its poor notices and box-office showing, *Sylvia Scarlett* was, for Grant, a personal triumph. "Cary Grant practically steals the picture," said *Variety*'s critic, echoing the opinions of both *The New York Post* and *Time* magazine, which added: "The film is made memorable by . . . Cary Grant's superb depiction of the cockney." For the first time on the screen, the actor had managed to convince his public that he was more than merely a handsome leading man. Grant didn't get the girl; Brian Aherne took that honor (once Hepburn had doffed trousers for skirts). But he *did* get the notices.

Grant's role in *Sylvia Scarlett* has drawn the comments of his colleagues. George Cukor has

SYLVIA SCARLETT (1936). With Katharine Hepburn and Edmund Gwenn.

SYLVIA SCARLETT (1936). With Katharine Hepburn, Dennie Moore and Edmund Gwenn.

been quoted, in Andrew Sarris's book, *Interviews with Film Directors:* "Up to then, he had been a rather handsome, rather wooden leading man. But suddenly, during the shooting, he felt all his talents coming into being—maybe because it was the first part which really suited his background. He suddenly burst into bloom. It produced a wonderful performance."[*] And Katharine Hepburn, in Gary Carey's *Cukor & Co.*, recalls: "It was Cary Grant's first decent part, because George knew Cary and cast him as a character comedian, which is what he made his career on. He was the only thing that really made a hit in *Sylvia Scarlett.*"[**]

After working with Cukor and Hepburn in an offbeat comedy-drama like *Sylvia Scarlett*, the thought of returning to more Paramount programmers did not sit well with Grant. At this juncture, Metro-Goldwyn-Mayer tried to obtain his services for a secondary lead in *Mutiny on the Bounty* opposite Clark Gable, but Paramount refused. Franchot Tone got the part—and an Academy Award nomination.

tratir
to loan
Harlow p
improbable
tic drama, the
cast Grant as a
André Charville, a da        la-
tor who marries Americ    show-
girl Suzy (Harlow), after a whirlwind romantic whirl. But André soon begins to stray with a glamorous spy, Madame Eyrelle (Benita Hume), whose henchmen ultimately kill him. At the film's close, Suzy and her old beau (Franchot Tone) contrive to make André's death seem noble by putting his body behind the controls of his cracked-up plane, thus providing a variation on *The Eagle and the Hawk*'s ending. To economize, *Suzy* utilized aerial footage from Howard Hughes' 1930 flying classic *Hell's Angels.*

Back at his home studio, Grant then made two comedies with Joan Bennett, *Big Brown Eyes* and *Wedding Present*, released six months apart in 1936. Of the pair, *Big Brown Eyes* is far and away the better, more entertaining picture, thanks to a witty script by Raoul Walsh and Bert Hanlon and snappy direction by Walsh, who had successfully guided Bennett through an equally tough, wisecracking role

[*] Andrew Sarris, *Interviews with Film Directors* (New York, 1969), p.74.

[**] Gary Carey, *Cukor & Co.*, (New York, p. 51)

*SUZY (1936). With Jean Harlow and Franchot Tone.*

*BIG BROWN EYES (1936). With Isabel Jewell and Joan Bennett.*

opposite Spencer Tracy in *Me and My Gal* (1932).

A comedy-melodrama about a detective (Grant) and a manicurist (Bennett) on the trail of jewel thieves and killers, *Big Brown Eyes* (a meaningless title) is part thriller and part "screwball" comedy. In one sequence, after there's a falling-out between them, Grant attempts to gain admittance to Bennett's apartment by arousing her jealous curiosity. His ruse: use his skill as a ventriloquist to conjure an imaginary female, with whom it *sounds* as though he's flirting. The falsetto voice used on the film's soundtrack obviously isn't Cary Grant's, but as he carries out a conversation with himself, he acts out both roles and, the scene is hilarious. Subsequently, having let Grant into her flat, Bennett pulls the same trick on *him* from behind her bathroom door. Cary walks out.

*Wedding Present* is decidedly inferior, a would-be farce that offers few laughs and seemingly endless silliness. This time, Joan Bennett plays a newspaper re-

WEDDING PRESENT (1936). With Joan Bennett.

*THE AMAZING QUEST OF ERNEST BLISS (1936). With Mary Brian.*

porter in love with an editor (Grant). Their marriage plans present so many obstacles that she decides to jilt him and call the whole thing off. In the heavy-handed proceedings that follow, Bennett becomes engaged to Conrad Nagel but she and Grant are finally reunited.

To the film's credit, director Richard Wallace takes the uninspired Joseph Anthony screenplay at a fast pace. The movie closes on a frantic note with Grant arranging to get Bennett "a real wedding present" in the form of a siren-blasting fire engine, on which they ride off. Here, producer B.P. Schulberg unwisely cuts costs to the extent

of using ancient street-scene footage showing antique cars and women in cloche hats, with speeded-up action that results in a rather disconcerting finale.

*Wedding Present* also ended Cary Grant's contract with Paramount. Politely but firmly, he informed the studio that he wasn't going to renew, on any terms; he wished to free-lance. Grant claims he was Hollywood's first free-lance actor and admits that it was a big step to take, adding, "Only Mae West and Marlene Dietrich were permitted to choose their parts at Paramount, and I was fed up with what I was doing. It didn't turn out too badly. Without a contract, I pushed my money up to $300,000 a picture in no time."

Grant's first choice of a freelance vehicle was a poor one. He returned to England for an ill-advised remake of E. Phillips Oppenheim's *The Amazing Quest of Ernest Bliss*, which had been a successful light-comedy vehicle for British stars Henry Edwards and Chrissie White in 1921. In the title role, Grant played a wealthy young idler who accepts a challenge that he can earn his own way for a year without using his money or connections. In the course of the story, Bliss works as a salesman, a grocer, and a chauffeur, and finds romance with a secretary (Mary Brian, another fugitive from a waning Hollywood career). Eventually, Bliss admits his wealthy background to the young lady to finance an operation that saves her sister's life. The ending is as expected: boy wins girl away from marriage to her boss.

The amateurish 1936 version of this Oppenheim yarn left much to be desired, under the uninspired direction of Alfred Zeisler, a fugitive from the UFA studios of Germany. In England, the film was also shown as *A Rich Young Man* while, in America, it has variously been known as *Romance and Riches*

and *Amazing Adventure*. Whatever its title, the movie was a failure in both countries.

From this dismal venture, Cary Grant returned to Hollywood and a pleasant surprise. Largely because of favorable public response to his performances in *Suzy* and *Sylvia Scarlett* there was a demand for his services that resulted in his signing joint contracts with both RKO and Columbia—with script approval. For the next seven years he would alternate almost exclusively between the two studios—picking and choosing the stories to which he was best suited. And, by 1936, Cary Grant was well aware of his talents, as well as his shortcomings.

*When You're in Love*, Grant's first film for Columbia, with its faint echoes of *Enter Madame*, gave little indication that his years at Columbia would be any more fortuitous than those with Paramount. Grace Moore was the picture's star—an Australian opera singer named Louise Fuller, who is stranded in Mexico when immigration authorities refuse to allow her entry into the U.S. By hiring itinerant artist Jimmy Hudson (Grant) to marry her, the diva gets across the border, with every intention of obtaining a subsequent divorce. But this marriage of con-

*WHEN YOU'RE IN LOVE (1937). With Grace Moore.*

venience eventually becomes the real thing.

Among the first of Metropolitan Opera prima·donnas to bring operatic music to the screen, Miss Moore had scored a huge success in the legendary *One Night of Love* (1934), a movie which paved the way for similar moves by her New York colleagues Lily Pons (*I Dream Too Much*, 1935) and Gladys Swarthout (*Rose of the Rancho*, 1936). They were not successful, but Grace Moore's blonde prettiness, easy charm, and vitality enhanced her popularity, and in *When You're in Love*, she was sufficiently wise to vary her generous sampling of arias with pop-concert numbers like "Siboney" (sung in Spanish) and even Cab

Calloway's "Minnie the Moocher." Although constantly upstaged by Miss Moore's vocal flings, Cary Grant brought the appropriate note of light comedy to his role. The screenplay was the work of Robert Riskin, then fresh from the highly popular *Mr. Deeds Goes to Town* (1936). For *When You're in Love*, Riskin also turned director—for the first and last time. Aline MacMahon, who played Grace Moore's secretary in the film, reports that, while making this film, Grant often said that he missed stage acting.

*The Toast of New York*, Grant's first film under his concurrent RKO contract, was a lavish example of ersatz Americana, focusing on the colorful lives of nineteenth century Wall Street tycoon Jim Fisk (Edward Arnold) and his mistress, the actress Josie Mansfield (Frances . Farmer). Grant played Nick Boyd, Fisk's loyal business partner who first joins forces with him in a fake medicine show just prior to the Civil War. Later, they build a fortune in the steamship business. The story's true romantic involvement appears to exist solely between Nick and Josie. At the fade-out, Fisk's assassination finally clears the path for their union.

As directed by Rowland V. Lee, *The Toast of New York* is lively, boisterous entertainment but, as history or biography, it is totally spurious, with writers Dudley Nichols, John Twist, and Joel Sayre substituting action and romance for fact, all with an overlay of irreverent humor. Edward Arnold appeared to be getting renewed mileage from his *Diamond Jim* characterization of two years previous, but the beautiful Miss Farmer, aware that the real Josie Mansfield had been a "designing harlot," battled vainly to portray this unpleasant character with an integrity lacking in the screenplay. In her shattering posthumous autobiography, *Will There Really Be a Morning?*, the actress reports that Cary Grant remained "undisturbed and unaffected" by her on-the-set temperament: "He remained polite but impersonal, and the prospects of another film with him created no

*THE TOAST OF NEW YORK (1937). With Frances Farmer.*

*TOPPER (1937). With Roland Young and Constance Bennett.*

interest for me, one way or another."°

Grant's next movie, *Topper*, offered the actor not only a delightful change of pace, but also a prophetic look at the upward course of his career as an expert light comedian. Made for independent producer Hal Roach, then releasing his product through MGM, this adaptation

°Frances Farmer, *Will There Really Be a Morning?* (New York, 1972), p.22.

of Thorne Smith's whimsical novel is both a classic "screwball" farce and a masterpiece of trick photography and sound effects. Comedy veteran Norman Z. McLeod, with whom Grant had briefly worked four years earlier in *Alice in Wonderland*, directed a hand-picked comedy cast that featured Constance Bennett, Roland Young, Billie Burke, and Alan Mowbray. The plot is simple and rife with possibilities well realized by its adaptors, Jack Jevne, Eric Hatch, and Eddie Moran: George and Marion Kerby (Grant and Bennett), a handsome and wealthy young couple given to a life of partying and pleasure, are killed in an auto crash, but return as spirits devoted to the rehabilitation of their friend, Cosmo Topper (Young), an inhibited and henpecked bank president whose dull, routine life they proceed to upset. Blessed with the ability to appear and disappear at will, the Kerbys playfully introduce Topper to the pleasure of champagne and their own hectic former life style.

Aided by skillful camera magic, Grant, Young, and Miss Bennett sustained an inspired level of sophisticated whackiness. Undoubtedly, much of *Topper*'s entertainment value derives from the expertise of cameraman Norbert Brodine and editor William Terhune, but without the deft performances of its cast, this ectoplasmic soufflé would flatten dismally. Grant and Bennett disport in top form as they participate in street brawls, introduce Young to the pleasures of Bacchus, or confound an incredulous hotel detective (Eugene Pallette) with their materializing act. Their antics are beautifully balanced by Roland Young's gradual emergence from milquetoast to man-about-town, a delineation so charming that it won the actor an Academy Award nomination

*TOPPER (1937). With Roland Young and Constance Bennett.*

as Best Supporting Actor. Despite faintly negative reviews, *Topper*, released at the height of America's craze for "screwball" comedy, became one of 1937's most popular movies. The following year, its success inspired a sequel, *Topper Takes a Trip*, in which Young and Miss Bennett philandered anew—but without Cary Grant, who was only seen in introductory "recap" footage from the original film, inserted for the benefit of those unfamiliar with the Topper phenomenon.

For Grant, *Topper* was a logical springboard to Columbia's *The Awful Truth* (1937), one of the enduring comedy classics of the screen, and the first of the actor's three happy associations with Irene Dunne, who had already proven herself a top-flight comedienne in *Theodora Goes Wild* (1936). Leo McCarey, whose credits ranged from the Marx Brothers (*Duck Soup*) and Mae West (*Belle of the Nineties*) to a touching drama of old age (*Make Way For Tomorrow*), directed this flippant tale about a divorcing couple, Lucy and Jerry Warriner, whose lives are complicated during the ninety-day interlocutory period, by visitation rights over their pet terrier, Mr. Smith (played by the wire-haired fox terrier best known as "Asta" in the *Thin Man* series). In one of this movie's hilarious slapstick scenes, Lucy tries vainly to keep the derby of a gentleman caller from Jerry's sight, while Mr. Smith's well-trained "retriever" talents inaugurate a

*THE AWFUL TRUTH (1937). With Ralph Bellamy and Irene Dunne.*

*THE AWFUL TRUTH (1937). With Irene Dunne.*

marvelously amusing game of hide-and-seek that poses a constant threat to her privacy.

The film's best comedy sequences rely on the visual and the physical, with Jerry making efforts to sabotage Lucy's romance with the rich but dull Daniel Leeson (Ralph Bellamy in a role he had virtually patented), and eventually winning back Lucy in a pajama-clad connecting-bedrooms sequence that successfully bypassed the Hays Office censors, thanks to the immaculate taste and timing of Dunne and Grant, under the guidance of Leo McCarey. (He won that year's Academy Award for his direction.) *The Awful Truth* garnered four other 1937 Oscar nominations, including Best Picture, Best Screenplay, and Irene Dunne—but, oddly enough, not Cary Grant. Nevertheless, the picture made him a top star.

Columbia next had set Grant and Jean Arthur for *The Pioneers* but, when that production was cancelled, he was free to accept a role that had already been turned down by no less than Ronald Colman, Robert Montgomery, and Ray Milland— the shy, dignified paleontologist who tangles with a madcap heiress in the delightfully daffy

*BRINGING UP BABY (1938). With Katharine Hepburn.*

*Bringing Up Baby* (1938), opposite Katharine Hepburn. The film's director, Howard Hawks, was an old hand at tough, rugged dramas *(Scarface, Barbary Coast)*, but had only one previous 1930s comedy to his credit—the 1934 John Barrymore-Carole Lombard farce, *20th Century*. With *Bringing Up Baby*, Hawks proved himself a versatile director, and Cary Grant obviously responded well to his creative guidance. More fortuitously cast this time than in *Sylvia Scarlett*, Grant and Hepburn proved a comedy team of chemical perfection.

*Bringing Up Baby*'s plot has little coherence. Dudley Nichols and Hagar Wilde, working from a short story by Wilde, obviously had great fun concocting this string of amusing comedy clichés and outrageously whacky situations, and the proceedings clearly provided a happy collaboration between cast and director. The movie centered on David Huxley (Grant), a repressed professor whose lifetime project—the reconstruction of a dinosaur skeleton—is totally disrupted by his encounters with Susan Vance (Hepburn), a wealthy young lady who owns a mischievous terrier named George, a pet leopard that answers to Baby—and a contagious penchant for getting into scrapes. When George makes off with the dinosaur's intercostal clavicle, a priceless bone David has just obtained to complete his work, the fun really begins. Dog buries bone; professor accompanies heiress into the Connecticut countryside; the pet leopard gets loose at the same time, coincidentally, that a dangerous cat escapes from the local zoo; David finds himself clad in Susan's negligee, and so on. Hawks and his writers failed to avoid one musty sight or sound gag in the proceedings, yet—with the aid of a brilliant cast (including such topnotch character actors as Charles Ruggles, May Robson, Barry Fitzgerald, and Walter Catlett) each new turn of the script seems fresh, inspired, and infectiously funny.

For Hepburn, *Bringing Up Baby* was a radical departure from the soap operas and costume dramas that helped get her named "box office poison." Under Hawks, she displayed an untapped knack for comic timing, and even slapstick, that gave her career a much-needed boost. Grant was on more familiar territory, and one recalls scene after scene in which he excels through the skill of a line reading or a facial nuance: upon unexpectedly greeting May Robson while dressed in a frilly negligée, he explains the situation with a frantic leap and an inspired reading of the line, "I went *gay* all of

*BRINGING UP BABY (1938). With Katharine Hepburn and Nissa.*

a sudden!" In a nightclub sequence with Hepburn, he struggles to maintain his dignity while helping the dizzy heiress hide the fact that she's torn her dress in back—by walking closely behind her as they shuffle for an exit. Or again, stumbling by night over the New England countryside with Hepburn, as they seek to locate the missing Baby by singing the animal's favorite tune, "I Can't Give You Anything But Love, Baby." The jail sequence, with most of the cast behind bars matching wits with Walter Catlett's excited constable, is another well remembered highlight. And the finale is equally mad: Grant mounts a high work platform to complete his dinosaur by attaching the missing clavicle—only to have his life's work collapse when Hepburn climbs up to join him.

Howard Hawks has explained how Grant developed the whinnying device he has occasionally deployed in comedy. "We have a scene in *Bringing Up Baby* where he's angry. I said, 'pretty dull. You get angry like Joe Doakes next door. Can't you think of somebody who gets angry and it's funny?' And then I remembered a man who practically whinnys like a horse when he's angry—so he did it."

*Holiday*, Grant's only other 1938 film, provides a marvelous balance to *Bringing Up Baby*. At Columbia, he and Hepburn continued their happy association from the RKO farce with an extraordinarily pleasing excursion into another form of humor—the comedy of manners. Philip Barry's 1928 play about the futility of riches had been filmed by Pathé in 1930 with Ann Harding, Robert Ames, and Mary Astor in the roles now essayed respectively by Hepburn, Grant, and Doris Nolan. Faced with mediocre scripts at RKO, Katharine Hepburn bought her way out of her contract with that studio expressly so that she could work again under George Cukor's direction. She wanted to play the role that she had understudied on Broadway ten years earlier—the nonconformist Linda Seton who convinces her snobbish sister Julia's fiancé Johnny (Grant) that he's better suited to *her*. Having met and fallen for the older sister (Nolan) at Lake Placid, this handsome and unconventional fellow arrives to meet the socially prominent New York Setons, and sets them on their stuffy heels with his theories about money and pleasure. It's his opinion that a man should retire while young for a long "holiday," to discover life and enjoy it while in his prime, returning to

*HOLIDAY (1938) . With Doris Nolan and Katharine Hepburn.*

*HOLIDAY (1938). With Katharine Hepburn.*

work in his *later* years. In embracing these radical notions, Linda realizes that she and Johnny are kindred souls, and she eventually wins him away from Julia, giving up her ivory-tower life for an unknown future with Johnny.

Donald Ogden Stewart and Sidney Buchman bolstered Barry's original play with so witty an adaptation that Cukor and a hand-picked cast could hardly fail. Literate, amusing, thought-provoking, and often quite moving, *Holiday* is a vintage film that admirably stands the test of time, glowing as brightly as ever some thirty-five years after its original release. The casting is perfection, from Grant and Hepburn through Jean Dixon and Edward Everett Horton as warm, wise old friends of Johnny's, to Henry Kolker, brilliant as the girls' stuffy, snobbish father, who wants Johnny to work in the Seton bank. The plot revolves about the charmingly rebellious Linda, and here Hepburn is at her loveliest and most vibrant. Opposite her, Grant's sincere, low-born but self-made Johnny awakens an innate sense of fun—and, indeed, conveys (as in *Bringing Up Baby*) a delicious sense of fun to the *audience*, as well. In a role that afforded him the opportunity to recall his Bob Pender days with some back-somersault acrobatics, the actor blends surface comedy with a layer of seriousness of purpose that's genuinely disarming. With his look of pained patience, Grant quite walks off with the movie, right from under Katharine Hepburn's talented nose.

George Cukor has said, "*Holiday* was a very happy picture to make," and the results would appear to bear him out.

Cary Grant's three 1939 films offered him a dramatic and interesting change of pace, although a vein of comedy runs through each of them. In *Gunga Din*, director George Stevens' rousing adventure yarn derived from Rudyard Kipling, Grant is the clown of his British regiment in India. In Howard Hawks' *Only Angels Have Wings* he is flip and grimly sarcastic as his fliers face danger and death to deliver the mails despite the onslaughts of nature. And, in the sudsy plot twists of *In Name Only*, Grant displayed charm and wit in the face of a loveless marriage to a shrew. In none of these films is Grant less than professional, nor does his expertise suffer from the demands of scripts sometimes calling for heavy and unbelievable melodramatics.

If *Gunga Din* is unbelievable, it most certainly isn't heavy, for this high-spirited romp through Kipling territory combines action and spectacle with a skill that belies George Stevens' contention that its filming was begun with an uncompleted script, and that some scenes were even improvised—an unusual situation in Hollywood filmmaking of the 1930s. Indeed, Stevens has revealed that the bugle scene between Grant and Sam Jaffe was devised on the spot. For his characterization in this blend of Kipling's title poem, his *Soldiers Three*, and an original story by Ben Hecht and Charles MacArthur, Cary Grant again turned cockney. Along with uncouth Victor McLaglen and dashing Douglas Fairbanks, Jr., Grant formed the humorous balance of a Dumas-like triumvirate: three inseparable sergeants battling the murderously fanatical Thugs in British India.

If Grant was occasionally stolid amid the triangular plot machinations of *The Last Outpost*, his previous excursion into embattled India, he is quite the antithesis in *Gunga Din*. And who could forget his clownish bravado when, surrounded by the cut-throat enemy, he brazenly marches in their midst, singing and whistling, and finally shouting, "You're all under arrest!" just before he's captured. Or his

GUNGA DIN (1939). With Eduardo Ciannelli, Victor McLaglen and Douglas Fairbanks Jr.

efforts to out-box the robust McLaglen!

George Stevens' then most recent excursions into small-town drama (*Alice Adams*), musicals (*Swing Time*, *A Damsel in Distress*), and comedy (*Vivacious*

*Lady)* gave little indication of the skill with which he would handle the spectacular heroics, humor, and tongue-in-cheek melodrama of *Gunga Din*. For this film, the thirty-five-year-old director also branched out to be-come his own producer, operating on an unheard of two-million-dollar budget, under the guidance of Pandro S. Berman. He-man heroics are kept to the fore, and even the occasional presence of women (chief among them, an

*GUNGA DIN (1939). With Ann Evers, Joan Fontaine and Douglas Fairbanks Jr.*

ingenuous Joan Fontaine, involved in a subsidiary romance with Fairbanks) is not allowed to seriously threaten a prevailing mood of red-blooded adventure. Photographed in panoramic black-and-white by Joseph H. August, this movie remains today much more colorful and entertaining than many a rainbow-hued derivative, notably its 1962 remake, *Sergeants 3*, with Frank Sinatra, Dean Martin, and Peter Lawford.

If *Only Angels Have Wings* is relatively familiar as adventure-dramas go, it is nonetheless entertaining. The setting is Barranca, port of call for South American banana boats and central point for a rickety airline that carries mail over the Andes. Grant portrays Jeff Carter, the tough boss of this tight-knit little colony of bachelor pilots, whose quarters are invaded first by showgirl Bonnie Lee (Jean Arthur), who falls hard for the rudely indifferent Jeff, then by the dishonored Bat McPherson (Richard Barthelmess), "the first pilot that ever bailed out of his plane and let his mechanic crash." The fact that McPherson's sensual young wife Judy (Rita Hayworth) arrives with him and, coincidentally, happens to be Jeff's ex-fiancée, provides predictable complications. Dangerous air missions and the obligatory bad weather added suspense to the screenplay by Jules Furthman, working from an original story that Hawks says he whipped together when Columbia production boss Harry Cohn suddenly ordered a film tailored for Grant and Miss Arthur.

In the capable hands of Jean Arthur, the clichéd stranded-entertainer ("I quit a show in Valparaiso") attains more human and likable dimensions than usual in such he-man dramas. The unusual mixture of innate toughness and childlike vulnerability so cunningly trademarked by this actress helps persuade us that an unconvincing romance between mismatched people could actually have a happy ending. "You're a queer duck," Jeff

ONLY ANGELS HAVE WINGS (1939). With Jean Arthur.

quips, to which Bonnie retorts, "So are you!" And later, when she decides to let her scheduled boat sail without her, thus confining her to the little community for another week, he rudely rejects her with "Look, I didn't ask you to stay." "I know," she replies. "You wouldn't ask *any* woman to do *anything*!"

As expected, Judy still carries a torch for Jeff, and it develops that her "happy" marriage to McPherson is anything but. In the fifth year of her movie career, Rita Hayworth displayed a sensual beauty and self-confidence that indicates an actress headed for stardom, although vocally she's still of the heavy-whisper school. The first scene in which she and Grant are left alone provokes the expected sparks, an exciting blend of actor-personality with brittle dialogue. "Surprised to find me married?" she taunts. "I thought you'd had enough of fliers," he answers. In a later scene between the two in a deserted hotel bar, he tells her off and douses her with water in the treat-'em-rough Cagney-Bogart manner.

Most memorable of all in the movie is the Hawksian milieu of a society dominated by men who brawl continuously and regularly risk their lives for their work. Despite the melodramatics of Furthman's plot, these portions ring the truest. Hawks himself has stated that most of this film's incidents are based on fact. Also worthy of note are the exciting aerial scenes for which Paul Mantz was chief flier and technical adviser.

John Cromwell's *In Name Only*, made for RKO in 1939, is a romantic tearjerker, but glossily produced and intelligently handled. Grant plays Alec Walker, wealthy but disillusioned by his marriage to Maida (Kay Francis), who wed him for money and position, and intends to cling to what she's attained. When he meets Julie Eden (Lombard), a young widow who's rented a cottage near his Connecticut estate, Alec falls in love with her. Maida seems agreeable to a divorce so that her husband can be free to marry Julie, and the lovers plan their future. But, upon her return from a trip to Paris, Maida reveals her true feelings, not only refusing to grant Alec the divorce, but stating that, should he bring suit, she'll then sue Julie for alienation of affection. That night Alec gets drunk and contracts pneumonia. As he recovers in the hospital, there's a confrontation between Julie and Maida that points to a brighter future for the two protagonists.

ONLY ANGELS HAVE WINGS (1939). With Allyn Joslyn, John Carroll, Rita Hayworth, Donald Barry, Richard Barthelmess and Louis Jean Heydt.

From this sudsy tale, well adapted by Richard Sherman from *Memory of Love*, a novel by Bessie Breuer, John Cromwell and an exceptional cast manage to suspend audience disbelief by understating the melodramatics and emphasizing the down-to-earth. In *The New York Times*, Bosley Crowther called *In Name Only*, "one of the most adult and enjoyable pictures of the season," adding, "It is particularly gratifying to encounter a film which does unblushingly tackle the hackneyed theme of husband, wife, and other woman, and which acknowledges by tactful implication a few of the facts of life."

For Francis and Lombard, cast against the type of role customarily offered them in that era, the film was a minor triumph. For Grant, it was little more than another opportunity to demonstrate how witty and charming a gentleman he is. In short, he just played himself.

In 1940, Cary Grant returned to comedy with *His Girl Friday* and *My Favorite Wife*, switched to historical drama in *The Howards of Virginia*, and played charming foil to Katharine Hepburn in the screen version of her Broadway hit, *The Philadelphia Story*. The first and last of these pictures are among the most fondly remembered

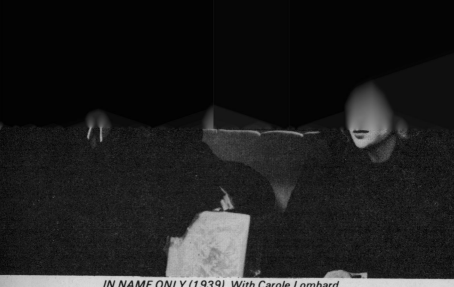

IN NAME ONLY (1939). With Carole Lombard.

(and often revived) from a golden era of Hollywood humor.

*His Girl Friday* first reached the public as *The Front Page*, a 1928 Broadway hit by Ben Hecht and Charles MacArthur. In 1931, Lewis Milestone directed the first film version of this hardy newspaper comedy, with Adolphe Menjou as hard-boiled editor Walter Burns, and Pat O'Brien making his motion picture debut in a re-creation of his stage role, star reporter Hildy Johnson.

For the 1940 Columbia remake, Howard Hawks devised the idea of making Hildy a *female* reporter and, with Ben Hecht's approval, he and screenwriter Charles Lederer "opened up" the play, devised additional gags, developed the new triangle situation between editor, star reporter, and reporter's fiancé—and emerged with one of the year's hit movies.

*His Girl Friday* presents Hildy Johnson (Rosalind Russell) as a retiring journalist, who has decided to give it all up to marry the dull but respectable Bruce Baldwin (Ralph Bellamy), and she pays a final visit to her former editor and ex-husband Walter Burns (Grant), who can't understand her reasons for giving up a successful career for married life in Albany. "He wants a home and children," smugly states Hildy. To which Walter retorts, "He sounds like a guy *I* ought to marry!" And immediately, *His Girl Friday* is off and

74

running, nonstop.

The plot takes us through newspaper crises, melodrama involving an escaped prisoner who's been sentenced to die for killing a policeman, an abandonment of marital plans, and Hildy's final decision that, although Bruce isn't for her, ex-husband Walter and the newspaper business definitely are!

In the hands of Grant and Russell, Walter and Hildy provide crackling good fun as they snap and bicker, lovingly toss vitriol and invective at each other, and display perfect teamwork in covering the scoop of the year. Hawks directs his stars and a brilliant cast of supporting actors (Gene Lockhart, Porter Hall, Billy Gilbert, John Qualen, Roscoe Karns, Abner Biberman, Alma Kruger, Regis Toomey, et al.) at such a breathless, staccato pace that it was once written that he demanded his cast deliver their lines at the rate of 240 words a minute! Hawks refutes this, explaining that he carefully worked it out so that speeches constantly overlapped, thus creating the *illusion* of increased pace. Nevertheless, once *His Girl Friday* starts, it never lets up, and sometimes approaches hysteria. At times, it seems as if the rapid-fire dialogue will be drowned out by the incessantly jangling telephones of its pressroom setting. Yet Hawks always keeps his film safely this side of chaos and his characters this side of complete exhaustion.

With that eternal sidelong glance and devilish twinkle in his eye, Cary Grant plays Walter Burns for the Machiavellian taskmaster he is. Taking his ex-wife and her blandly pleasant fiancé out to a restaurant, he inquires, "Are you going to live with your mother?" "Well, just for the first year," replies Bruce. "How—nice!" quips Walter (with all the irony at Grant's command), then, half musing to himself: "A home —in Albany!"

In the climactic scene, in which Grant and Russell compete vocally on separate telephones, he breaks into a whinny —a habit the actor would sometimes fall back on in farce. And here, for a moment, the dialogue takes a turn for the improvisational as Grant responds to another actor's line with: "The last person to say that to me was Archie Leach, just before he cut his throat!" Hawks admits that there was a lot of ad-libbing in *His Girl Friday*. "There is in every picture that's any good," he says. "You write a story up in a room. With a good actor, the thing comes alive when you get to a set. The actor contributes things,

*HIS GIRL FRIDAY (1940). With Ralph Bellamy and Rosalind Russell.*

*HIS GIRL FRIDAY (1940). With Frank Jenks, Roscoe Karns, Gene Lockhart, Porter Hall, Alma Kruger, Rosalind Russell, Regis Toomey and Cliff Edwards.*

and you think of things for the actor to do—some of the best lines come then, or after you finish the picture."

For RKO's *My Favorite Wife*, Grant was reunited with Irene Dunne in a hilarious variation on the old *Enoch Arden* theme. He played a widower who remarried (Gail Patrick), only to have his new life disrupted by the return of his old wife (Dunne) who, long presumed lost at sea, has spent the past seven years on a desert island with a virile young scientist (Randolph Scott). Garson Kanin, who had just directed Ginger Rogers in *Bachelor Mother*, refused to be intimidated by the fact that this film's *producer* was the same Leo McCarey who had worked wonders with Grant and Dunne in their previous hit, *The Awful Truth*. Although McCarey had intended to direct *My Favorite Wife* himself, the injuries he had incurred in a serious auto accident necessitated relinquishing the directorial reins to young Kanin.

The script derived from a story idea by McCarey, but really came into flower under the combined wit of Samuel and Bella Spewack, then best known for their play and movie, *Boy Meets Girl*. Despite the recent appearance of a similar theme in

*MY FAVORITE WIFE (1940). With Irene Dunne.*

Columbia's 1940 comedy, *Too Many Husbands*, this top-notch writing team brought forth an extraordinarily funny screenplay that won them an Academy Award nomination.

As the long-separated couple who battle a succession of mixed emotions and misunderstandings before reuniting for the fade-out, Dunne and Grant again proved their right to be called two of the screen's best farceurs. Dunne with her insinuating laughter and irresistible glances; and Grant with his suspicious eyes and bewildered mien made a delicious team of polished professionals working in

*MY FAVORITE WIFE (1940). With Irene Dunne and Chester Clute.*

perfect harmony. These two actors are a joy to watch as they struggle to extricate themselves from comedy situations which seem hopelessly complicated. And, as usual with films of that era, those in support were just right. Gail Patrick plays the extraneous new wife with the silky elegance she patented, and Scott has just the right look and manner to make even a 1940 audience wonder whether tradition might not reverse itself and let him win Irene Dunne away from Cary Grant. Of no less comedy impact is character actor Granville Bates, in his last role, as the harassed but acidulous judge who demands of Grant, "Where

did you go to school?" "Harvard," comes the answer, brought up short by the judge's baleful throwaway retort, "I'm a *Yale* man myself."

Frank Lloyd's *The Howards of Virginia*, filmed by Columbia in 1940, offered Cary Grant a rare excursion into historical narrative. Sidney Buchman's screenplay was based on the first part of Elizabeth Page's epic novel *The Tree of Liberty*, and the results veer uneasily between an engrossing, if superficial, Revolutionary War saga, highlighted by great moments in history, and a ponderous family narrative, characterized by more talk than action. The critics were divided over the film's merits. In *The New York Times*, Bosley Crowther called it "one of the best historical pictures to date," and praised Martha Scott, as the Tidewater aristocrat who marries a Virginia backwoodsman (Grant), as well as the wealth of period detail captured by Lloyd, who staged some location scenes in restored Williamsburg. But Crowther echoed a number of his fellow critics in his disappointment with Cary Grant: "There is a familiar comic archness about his style which is disquieting in his present serious role, and he never quite overcomes a bumptiousness which is distinctly annoying." Brief scenes from *The Howards of Virginia* were later used for the 1941 compilation film *Land of Liberty*, a salute to our national heritage originally shown at the 1939 World's Fair, but later revised and re-edited for theaters.

*The Philadelphia Story*, filmed at MGM in 1940, is a classic comedy that represents the perfect blend of cast, director, script, and handsome production values. (Joseph L. Mankiewicz was the producer.) Philip Barry's hit 1939 play had been especially tailored for the considerable talents of Katharine Hepburn, who had bought movie rights to the comedy, and who, in turn, sold them to MGM in a package deal that included her services as its star, George Cukor as director, and Cary Grant and James Stewart as her costars. To get

*THE HOWARDS OF VIRGINIA (1940). With Richard Carlson and Martha Scott.*

Grant, MGM agreed to give him top billing (over Hepburn) and pay his salary to British War Relief. They also gave him a choice of the two top male roles—the wealthy ex-husband or the canny reporter from *Spy* magazine. He chose the former, and Stewart played the latter—and won an Academy Award for his performance.

In this brittle comedy of manners about a lofty society girl who learns humility and understanding, Philip Barry offered not only a brilliant vehicle for Katharine Hepburn, but also a witty, entertaining follow up to his *Holiday*. For the film version, Donald Ogden Stewart, a friend of Barry's, expanded the play and took it out of the confines of its four walls, always remaining true to the Barry style of writing, dialogue, and character. In *The Philadelphia Story*, language is of the utmost importance, but so is characterization, and Cukor wisely allows his well-chosen cast to color their roles with the flavor of originality.

The plot is as enjoyable today as it was in 1940: Tracy Lord (Hepburn), socially prominent and "unapproachable" elder daughter of the Philadelphia Lords, is about to marry respectable-but-dull George Kittredge (John Howard). Into their Main Line estate, courtesy of Tracy's alcohol-prone ex-husband C.K. Dexter Haven (Grant), comes Mike Connor (Stewart) and Liz Imbrie (Ruth Hussey), respectively, a reporter and photographer from *Spy* magazine, a muckraking publication Tracy detests. In the course of twenty-four hours, the self-assured Tracy is twice toppled from her pedestal, first by the down-to-earth Mike, with whom she shares a delightfully tipsy evening (and midnight swim), then by her still-adoring former husband, who hides his affection behind a facade of insults and irreverent charm. (Her pool scene with Mike has a fascinatingly romantic aura that has kept it one of the screen's best-remembered moments.) When George, disturbed by his fiancée's behavior on the eve of her wedding, jilts her, Tracy decides to go through with the ceremony anyway. Faced with two last-minute suitors, Dexter and Mike (who really loves Liz), Tracy decides that she and Dexter should start over again.

Although *The Philadelphia Story* is really "The Tracy Lord Story," Cukor doesn't give Hepburn *all* the limelight. Under his guidance, the cast works together in a smoothly meshing ensemble, and everyone is exactly right,

*THE PHILADELPHIA STORY (1940). With James Stewart and Ruth Hussey.*

*THE PHILADELPHIA STORY (1940). With Katharine Hepburn and John Howard.*

from the top-name players to the marvelous child actress, Virginia Weidler, as Tracy's worldly, pleasantly precocious sister, to Roland Young as the carefree, skirt-chasing Uncle Willie. And Cary Grant plays C.K. Dexter Haven to perfection, striking just the right balance between sincerity and flippancy. "You never had any understanding of my deep and gorgeous thirst," he tells Tracy. Re-reviewing the film twenty-one years later in the *London Observer*, critic Penelope Gilliatt wrote of the film's stars: "All three give performances of such calm comic judgment that one wonders whether Cukor's legendary reputation as an actress's director does him honour enough."

When Mike asks him how Tracy met Kittredge, Dexter replies bitingly, "*Heaven* brought them together, I imagine!" And later, in one of the film's slickest exchanges of dialogue:

Kittredge: (stuffily) "A man expects his wife to be———"
Tracy (cutting in): "To behave herself. Naturally."
Dexter (almost an echo): "To behave herself naturally." (Kittredge gives him a dirty look).
Dexter: "Sorry."

*The Philadelphia Story* won Hepburn the New York Film Critics' Best Actress Award for 1940. In the Academy Award sweepstakes, she lost out to Ginger Rogers' *Kitty Foyle*, although her vehicle picked up Oscars for both Stewarts, actor and screenwriter.

Unfortunately, this film marked an untimely end to Cary Grant's happy association with both Cukor and Hepburn. Hepburn speaks fondly of Grant as "a delicious personality who has learned to do certain things marvelously well." And she adds, "He has a lovely sense of timing and an amusing face and lovely voice."

Back at Columbia for *Penny Serenade* (1941), Cary Grant gave a performance that drew an Academy Award nomination— his first. (Gary Cooper was the winner for *Sergeant York*). Seldom has a basically sentimental tearjerker been handled with such honesty and skill, balancing beautifully between laughter and tears. This heartwinning study of a young married couple named Julie and Roger (Grant and Irene Dunne), whose union crumbles after the loss of their adopted child, is told mainly in flashback form, as Julie plays old phonograph records. She recalls how they met, courted, married, and honeymooned in Tokyo, where she lost her expected baby dur-

*PENNY SERENADE (1941). With Irene Dunne.*

*PENNY SERENADE (1941). With Leonard Wiley and Irene Dunne.*

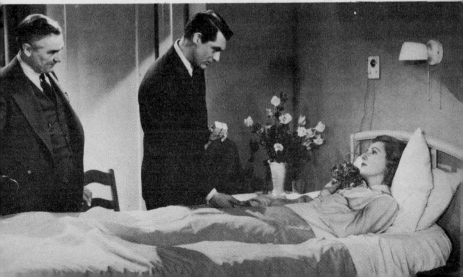

ing an earthquake ("The one thing I wanted I'm never going to have."). Later, there's the moving nursery scene in which Julie and Roger meet the child they will adopt. When Roger's change of fortune means that they can no longer afford the child—that they must return her to the adoption home—they are overwrought. In his most eloquent and touching scene, Grant appeals to a judge to let him keep little Trina: "I didn't know babies were so little." He wins the child back, but she later dies, and Roger leaves home in despair. In the story's hopeful ending, a new child from the home brings the couple together again.

Out of this seemingly bathetic tale, writer Morrie Ryskind and director George Stevens (in a change of pace from *Gunga Din*, his previous Grant film) work pure magic. Despite all the lachrymose plot twists to which this unfortunate young couple is subjected, the results are poignant and believable. In a triumph of taste, talent, and style over subject matter, Stevens keeps his stars on a thin but firm tightrope, never allowing them to take a fatal step in the wrong direction. It is also a particular tribute to Grant and Dunne that they bring it all off with such charm and intelligence. Charac-

ter actor Edgar Buchanan gives them solid support as their best friend in need, and Beulah Bondi reveals an orphanage matron as sensitive as she is sensible. *Penny Serenade* is the rare movie that gives "sentiment" a good name.

RKO's 1941 suspense drama, *Suspicion* marked Cary Grant's first appearance in an Alfred Hitchcock film, of which there would be four. The director has called Grant one of his favorite leading actors. In this, their first collaboration, Hitchcock realized a story problem on which he regrets having been forced by RKO to compromise. In the original novel, Francis Iles' *Before the Fact* (the movie's title during production), a naive young Englishwoman comes to realize that the charming fellow she's married is really a murderer. In the end, because of her love for him, she even allows him to kill her. But RKO refused to let Cary Grant be a killer. Consequently, in an unbelievable ending, Grant's suspicious actions during most of the foregoing film are inadequately explained away in time for a pat, happy ending.

Hitchcock reports how an RKO producer went behind his back to make sizable cuts in the final print so as to delete scenes implying Grant's guilt. But when the end result ran only fifty-five minutes, the director persuaded RKO's chief how ludicrous this was, and the deleted footage was restored.

From the start of Grant's relationship with Joan Fontaine, we suspect he's not what he seems. Later, when they're married and set up in elegant surroundings, she finds he has sold a pair of rare antique chairs that were a gift from her father (Sir Cedric Hardwicke). "Are you broke?" she inquires, to which he replies with customary Grant charm, "Monkey Face, I've been broke all my life." (And Fontaine registers that apprehensive amalgam of fear and anxiety that was often her most effective acting device.)

The screenplay, a collaboration between Samson Raphaelson, Joan Harrison, and Hitchcock's wife, Alma Reville, deliberately confuses the film's audience. Indeed, it seems destined that Grant *must* be a killer. Hitchcock shrewdly creates the atmosphere of a storybook English village not far from the threatening cliffs of Sussex, which appear to be an appropriate setting for the heroine's untimely demise. In one suspenseful sequence, Grant moodily drives Fontaine, at an alarming speed, along the coast road.

*SUSPICION (1941).*
*With Joan Fontaine.*

When her cliffside door falls open, it is impossible to tell whether Grant is attempting to push her out or hold her back. Although the latter is actually the case, the moment is characteristically ambivalent. Nor are we aided when he asks her, after her father's funeral: "Lina, do you ever have any regrets that you married me?" "Why do you ask that?" she counters. And he replies, "Well, it's obvious that your father would have left you a lot more money if you *hadn't* married me."

Two memorable *Suspicion* sequences linger in memory. In one brilliant montage, Joan Fon-

*SUSPICION (1941). With Joan Fontaine.*

taine's anagram game spells out the word "murder," juxtaposed with Grant's conversation with his friend (Nigel Bruce) about examining some cliffside real estate sites early the next morning. On a close-up of her frightened face, Hitchcock superimposes the camera-tilted shot of a high cliff, where the figure of a man is seen pushing another off the edge to his death, as the sea crashes on the rocks below. Fontaine, imagining the victim to be Nigel Bruce, faints to the floor.

Equally famed is the sequence in which Grant brings a glass of milk, which may or may not be poisoned, to Fontaine's bedside. Hitchcock claims he put a small light inside the milk glass to make it more luminous. For all the fakery of its suspense scenes and its obvious, studio-built village scenery, *Suspicion* remains effective and grimly amusing Hitchcock. In a role far more consistent, sympathetic and persuasive than Grant's, Joan Fontaine gave so charming a display of emotional range—from shyness to concern, joy, sadness, distrust, and ultimate fear for her life—that she won the 1941 Academy Award as Best Actress. It has often been said that this award was a belated nod to her possibly more impressive acting as *another* frightened heroine, in Hitchcock's 1940 classic, *Rebecca*.

It is not too widely known that *Arsenic and Old Lace*, released by Warner Brothers in the autumn of 1944, was completed nearly three years earlier. Although Warners was then known often to stockpile completed films and hold them up for many months, the reason for this movie's public delay was contractual: no film version could be released until after completion of the play's successful Broadway run. Producer-director Frank Capra saw, and fell in love with, this "wholesome black comedy," and when he found that it had already been sold to Warners, he worked out a package deal with Jack Warner. Josephine Hull and Jean Adair, who played the dear but homicidal old ladies around whom the farce revolved, could be borrowed from the Broadway play, but only if filming were accomplished during their four-week vacation from the show. But a star name was needed to sell *Arsenic and Old Lace* to motion picture audiences, and Capra persuaded Warner to meet the $100,000 asking price of Cary Grant, whom the director considered "Hollywood's greatest farceur." (Reportedly, Grant again gave his salary to War Relief charities.) Finally, the actual shooting was managed in the necessary four weeks—in the studio.

Joseph Kesselring's play is very much an ensemble effort, depending on the combined skill and timing of its cast, rather than offering any single actor a "star vehicle." For the screen version, Capra felt it necessary to embellish the play, as well as build up the role of theatrical critic Mortimer Brewster (the play's only sane character) to fit the star status of Cary Grant. To accomplish this, he secured the services of the seasoned comedy writing team, Julius J. and Philip G. Epstein, who had just completed for Warners a very successful screen adaptation of the George S. Kaufman-Moss Hart farce, *The Man Who Came to Dinner*. However, this time, the Epsteins became overly creative, introducing the film with a melee at Ebbets Field that had little to do with the story, followed by some romantic business involving Mortimer and his fiancée, Elaine (Priscilla Lane), trying without success, to avoid reporters and obtain their marriage license. This is followed by some romantic nip-ups in a cemetery adjoining their respective homes and, *finally*, we get down to the Kesselring plot.

*Arsenic and Old Lace* is the delightfully daffy tale of two elderly spinsters who maintain an old house in Brooklyn where they harbor a pleasantly deranged nephew who thinks he's Teddy Roosevelt, and indulge in their fondest pastime— sending lonely old gentlemen to an untimely but painless demise with a hearty dose of their homemade elderberry wine. In fact, when the play begins, they have already dispatched an even dozen, and buried them in the cellar. The situation is gruesome, but only in essence, for Kesselring treats it with delightful whimsy, enabling the audience to enjoy the proceedings thoroughly, while not believing them for a moment. The Epsteins maintained this borderline of good taste, as did Capra, although the latter frequently allows his more farcical scenes to be overplayed.

On the stage, Mortimer Brewster is a cynical critic of the George Jean Nathan school. And despite the fact that he has a fiancée, Elaine is the one who's doing the pursuing, as Mortimer has little use for women. The movie changes all that, building up Mortimer's scenes with his pixilated aunts and with his sinister, long-lost brother Jonathan (Raymond Massey), who's wanted by the law and seeks to hide

*ARSENIC AND OLD LACE (1941-1944). As Mortimer Brewster.*

*ARSENIC AND OLD LACE (1941-1944). With Peter Lorre, Raymond Massey, Josephine Hull, Priscilla Lane and Jean Adair.*

out in the Brewster home while his nervous surgeon-friend Dr. Einstein (Peter Lorre) performs facial plastic surgery on him.

Under Capra's guidance, Cary Grant plays this macabre comedy at a fast and frantic pace that mounts from a legitimate level of farce (his incredulous triple-take discovery that there's a body in the window seat) to a state of total abandon that throws all restraint to the winds in a shameless display of facial mugging, physical leaping about,

eye-popping, bellowing, and dithering hysteria. As his performance loses restraint, it reduces audience enjoyment, and becomes extremely tiring to watch. In contrast, both the Misses Hull and Adair maintain a delicious sense of quietly insane fun, as does John Alexander, also re-creating his Broadway role as the Teddy Roosevelt character. *Arsenic and Old Lace* is clever hokum, and when it finally reached theaters in 1944, audiences flocked to see it.

Back at Columbia, Cary Grant worked for the third and last time under George Stevens' direction in the curiously engaging comedy-drama entitled *The Talk of the Town*. In this odd mixture of farce and political theory written by Irwin Shaw and Sidney Buchman, Grant plays Leopold Dilg, a small-town radical ("the town malcontent") who has escaped from prison on a false murder charge. He hides out in the home of schoolteacher Nora Shelley (Jean Arthur) on the very evening her summer tenant, privacy-prone law professor Michael Lightcap (Ronald Colman) arrives. These three eventually form a romantic triangle in a plot that has Arthur persuade Colman to defend Grant.

This is an offbeat film for Stevens, and he frequently meets the demands of an uneven script with sly, farcical touches reminiscent of Frank Capra. Certainly, his trio of polished stars work wonders in maintaining audience interest in this battle between classicism and populism, in what some would term 118 minutes of sugarcoated message, as epitomized, perhaps, by a climactic speech of Colman's: "The law must be engraved in our hearts and practiced every minute—for our neighbors, as well as ourselves." Abandoning his custom-

# DOWNS AND UPS
# (1942-1948)

ary double-breasted suits for dark turtlenecks and an occasional dishevelled look, Grant is amusing yet forceful. Reacting to Colman's self-contained rhetorical professor, he states: "Some people write novels. Some people write music. I make speeches on street corners." Later, when Dilg spots his own "Wanted" poster in a Boston post office, he comments jauntily to Colman and Arthur, "No one would recognize me from that. Doesn't catch the spirit!"

Although Stevens allows his audience to believe that Arthur and Colman will end up together, he effects a last-minute reversal that is as unexpected as it is amusing. After Colman's law-and-order speech in Washington, where he has been appointed to the Supreme Court, Dilg gets up to leave and Nora rushes out to have a last word with him before he departs from their lives forever. He kisses her, mumbling, "See ya sometime," and off he goes, only to return and embrace her. They walk off together.

Curious though it is as a

film, *The Talk of the Town* was both a critical and commercial success, although Bosley Crowther thought that Grant's "casualness" was "slightly disturbing." The movie won no awards, but gathered seven Oscar nominations, including Best Picture and Best Screenplay.

The failure of Cary Grant's marriage to Virginia Cherrill had not exactly retired the actor to monkdom. Indeed, he had been rumored romantically serious

worth heiress Barbara Hutton, who had been married and divorced twice before. They began to see one another frequently and, during much of 1941, they were usually together when he wasn't engaged in filmmaking. On July 8, 1942, they were quietly married in the actor's garden. It was later disclosed that Grant had signed a paper relinquishing any claim to her money, should they ever divorce. Just before the ceremony, Cary Grant officially became an American citizen and had his name legally changed from Archibald Alexander Leach.

Outstanding films under top directors had helped give Grant steady box-office popularity. In the 1940s, moviegoing audiences generally supported *any* picture in which their favorites appeared, regardless of the work's merits. Consequently, with movies ground out of the major studios on an assembly-line basis, many mediocre films flowed in and out of the nation's theaters with scant complaint from most audiences. The fact that many of the films in which Cary Grant now chose to appear were below his former standards did little damage to his career.

He was next seen opposite Ginger Rogers, for the first time, in Leo McCarey's *Once Upon a*

about various Hollywood actresses, including Mary Brian, Ginger Rogers, and, especially, starlet Phyllis Brooks. In 1940, courtesy of the socially prominent partygiver, Countess Dorothy di Frasso, Grant met Wool-

*THE TALK OF THE TOWN (1942). With Jean Arthur.*

*Honeymoon* (1942), an inconsequential blend of comedy and drama set against the noncomedic background of war-torn Europe. In this uneven RKO film, written by McCarey and Sheridan Gibney, Grant was a U.S. news reporter, stationed in Warsaw during the bombing, who falls for an American stripper (Rogers) who has naively married a Nazi leader (Walter Slezak), an advance-man for Hitler. Subsequently, Grant rescues Rogers, and they join forces, breezing through Belgium, Holland, and Norway, with a bit of espionage in Paris for a climax.

Grant and Rogers play well together, and some of their comedy scenes display a sense of expert timing and enjoyment, he with his arch charm, and she with her brassy cunning. But McCarey misguidedly introduces moments of grim tragedy which mix uneasily and tastelessly with the comedy. In the midst of the horrors of World War II, he has his hero and heroine flit about the ruins of Warsaw, where they are mistaken for Jews and are, briefly, confined to a concentration camp. The mournful prayer for the dead, which echoes throughout the camp, makes the comic banter which preceded it sound very hollow indeed. *Once Upon a Honeymoon* (the title underscores this film's air of mis-placed gaiety) is a slick and well-played, but negligible, comedy.

Cary Grant's only 1943 movie, RKO's *Mr. Lucky*, was another breezy, romantic comedy-drama casting him in the type of part better suited to a George Raft—that of a heel gambler called Joe the Greek, whose less-than-exemplary activities include avoiding the draft and attempting to bilk money from a charity organization. But his character undergoes an abrupt change when he meets and falls in love with Dorothy Bryant (Laraine Day), a society girl who considers Joe a rough diamond. He then helps them raise the money necessary to send a relief ship overseas, and survives a double cross by a member of his mob.

Cary Grant plays all this with his accustomed air of light charm, whether reluctantly joining Florence Bates and the charity ladies in a knitting class or delivering a haymaker to his leading lady to save her from a bullet. The Milton Holmes-Adrian Scott screenplay also gave him a running gag involving the employment of cockney rhyming-slang ("Hand me my fiddle-faddle," meaning his best suit, etc.). This slight fable was pleasantly directed by H.C. Potter.

**ONCE UPON A HONEYMOON (1942). With Ginger Rogers.**

*MR. LUCKY (1943). With Florence Bates.*

*DESTINATION TOKYO (1944). With Warner Anderson.*

In 1944, the actor's career took a more serious turn, affording him strong roles in Warner Brothers' war film *Destination Tokyo* and RKO's *None But the Lonely Heart*, with the light whimsy of Columbia's *Once Upon a Time* sandwiched in the middle for variety.

*Destination Tokyo* marked the directorial debut of Delmer Daves, whose writing credits had included *Love Affair*, *Stage Door Canteen*, and *You Were Never Lovelier*. Grant, who now had both script and director approval, consented to let Daves direct the screenplay he and Albert Maltz had written, because he admired the writer's previous work and because he likes to help those whom he thinks deserve it. The gamble paid off with an exciting action melodrama whose then considerable length (135 minutes) did not detract from its entertainment value.

Grant, his usual mannerisms subdued, played the grim-faced commander of the U.S.S. Copperfin, a submarine charged with a perilous mission from San Francisco to Tokyo Bay: landing an observation party only a few hours before the American bombing. The sub becomes the target of enemy aircraft in the Aleutians, gets a bomb lodged in

her deck (it's defused in a suspenseful sequence), braves a Japanese mine field getting into Tokyo Bay, and suffers a terrific depth-bombing. Crew crises include an emergency appendectomy performed under inadequate conditions.

In *The New York Times*, Bosley Crowther called *Destination Tokyo*, "a big but too extravagant action film," although he approved the "slick, manly performances" of Grant, John Garfield, Alan Hale, and Dane Clark. Aside from one actress (Faye Emerson) in a small role, the movie wasted little time on romance. Underscoring the danger and suspense was a good score by Franz Waxman. *Destination Tokyo* remains among Hollywood's best films about submarine warfare.

*Once Upon a Time* (1944), originally filmed under the title of its original Norman Corwin-Lucille Fletcher Herrmann radio play, *My Client Curley*, is an odd little fable about the exploitation of a boy who has a pet dancing caterpillar. Originally, Columbia had scheduled it for Humphrey Bogart and Rita Hayworth, until the latter wisely rejected it as a film that would do nothing for her career. Instead, Columbia contract player Janet Blair played the trivial role of

*ONCE UPON A TIME (1944). With Ted Donaldson and Janet Blair.*

chorus girl Jeanne Thompson whose kid brother Pinky (Ted Donaldson) is the lad with Curley, the fabulous caterpillar, which he keeps in a shoebox, and which dances when the boy plays "Yes Sir, That's My Baby" on his harmonica.

Grant was characteristically arch as Jerry Flynn, the Broadway producer who is losing his theater after too many flops, and who hopes to make a fortune by selling Pinky's pet. But the lad refuses; he claims he can talk to his friend Curley and that one just doesn't *sell* one's *friend!*

Radio broadcaster Gabriel Heatter then gets wind of the story, and publicizes the Pinky-Curley situation as "a fairy tale come to life." Walt Disney becomes interested in using Curley in a film that will have an animated background. Again, Pinky refuses, but Jerry betrays him by promising the dancing worm to Disney for $100,000, one hundred times what they had offered to pay. Then Curley disappears, eventually reappearing in Pinky's apartment—in the form of a butterfly.

Director Alexander Hall keeps this slight situation from

becoming too sticky, while young Ted Donaldson steals the movie with his straightforward innocence, round little face, and childish treble. Fortunately, Curley the caterpillar is never shown —until later, when he flies out of the piano as a butterfly. However, in the climactic butterfly sequence, animation is used, creating an abrasive quality that distorts the film's fragile charm. As a radio play, *My Client Curley* may have had some appeal; elongated to fill a feature-length movie, it's mostly heavy-handed whimsy.

Grant now played a role that he had coveted—Ernie Mott, the cockney-tramp hero of Richard Llewellyn's best-selling novel, *None But the Lonely Heart,* a 1944 RKO film that won critical superlatives but scant audience support. It is a much subtler, more complex Cary Grant we see in this moody, haunting tale of a free-spirited drifter and his impoverished, ailing Ma (Ethel Barrymore) amid the dull oppressiveness of prewar London's East End. Playwright Clifford Odets crafted an intense but sensitive adaptation of the book— and was permitted to make his screen debut as its director. There was little dispute that Odets had done wonders to preserve the rich atmosphere and

brittle, poetic language of Llewellyn's book. That he had reinforced these qualities with a rare but knowing excursion into film directing was amazing. An occasional bit of staginess in the action did not appreciably detract from either mood or event. (Odets' only other film was *The Story on Page One*, which he directed, from his own screenplay, for Fox in 1959.)

As a character, Ernie Mott is a far cry from Jimmie Monkley, Grant's previous cockney of *Sylvia Scarlett*. Ernie's a disreputable fellow, whose cheap, flashy arrogance masks a basically poetic soul. Despite his restless wanderings, he's oddly, genuinely fond of his mother, an affection that leads him to crime, in an effort to better their lot. Ernie's search for another kind of love is no less ill-fated, as evidenced by his relationship with the appealing Ada (June Duprez). *None But the Lonely Heart* displays a sad, singing tragedy of the human condition, and Cary Grant's confused, undisciplined Ernie Mott is nothing short of brilliant in its complexities. Again, his performance won the actor an Academy Award nomination, and again he lost—this time to Bing Crosby's sympathetic priest of *Going My Way*. Heading a notable supporting

**NONE BUT THE LONELY HEART (1944). As Ernie Mott.**

cast that included Barry Fitzgerald, Jane Wyatt, George Coulouris, Dan Duryea, and Roman Bohnen, Ethel Barrymore won that year's Best Supporting Actress Oscar for her glowing Ma Mott.

Grant made no films in 1945. But in August of that year, his marriage to wealthy Barbara Hutton ended in divorce. Somehow, the divergent worlds of the leisurely rich and the working movie star created differences that were irreconcilable. As has been widely reported, Cary Grant and Barbara Hutton have remained on the best of terms—as he has apparently done with three of his four ex-wives.

Grant was next seen as himself, dancing briefly with Claudette Colbert in her 1946 comedy, *Without Reservations*, an unbilled visual gag, performed while he made another picture on the RKO lot. He starred in two films that year: *Night and Day*, a highly fictitious Cole Porter biography, and *Notorious*, a return engagement with suspense master Alfred Hitchcock.

Released amid the mid-1940s rash of musical biographies, *Night and Day* paid little heed to the factual details of the songwriter's life, but offered enough lilting Porter tunes and production polish to satisfy undemanding audiences. Alexis Smith was on hand in the largely fictional role of Porter's wife Linda, heading a large and impressive cast that included, as themselves, old Porter friends Monty Woolley and Mary Martin (singing "My Heart Belongs to Daddy").

Facetiously, Cole Porter had suggested to the brothers Warner that they get Cary Grant to play him on the screen—which they did, to the tune of $150,000. And so Grant, faced with a predictably phony screenplay by Charles Hoffman, Leo Town-

*NONE BUT THE LONELY HEART (1944). With Ethel Barrymore.*

*NIGHT AND DAY (1946). With Jane Wyman and Monty Woolley.*

send, and William Bowers, fell back on his stock-in-trade charm and sophistication. And he even got to sing "An Old-Fashioned Garden," "Miss Otis Regrets" with Monty Woolley, and "You're the Top" with Ginny Simms. In one particularly laughable sequence, accompanied by the meshing sounds of falling rain and a loudly ticking clock, he composes "Night and Day" to echoes of "You, you, you." Alexis Smith somehow manages to keep a straight face while Grant shouts, "Wait a minute! I think I've got it."

Grant's style considerably impressed Miss Smith, who reports: "The first scene I played with Cary Grant, I was standing under some mistletoe and he kissed me and I forgot I had the next line. I mean, when he looks at you and says, 'I love you,' he is so intense. You forget you have a function in the scene."

Cary Grant's first Technicolor film, *Night and Day*, was directed by Michael Curtiz, a demanding tyrant for whom Grant held little affection. Indeed, once filming was completed, the actor delivered himself of a well-articulated blast that startled Hollywood. "Mike," said Cary, "now that the last foot of this film is shot, I want you to know that if I'm ever stupid enough to be caught working with you, you'll know I'm either broke or I've lost my mind. You may bamboozle crews and cameramen to work with you, but not me, not again." Curtiz thought Grant was jesting, but the actor was entirely serious.

Hitchcock's *Notorious* marked the actor's first teaming with Ingrid Bergman, a lady with whom Grant has long maintained a close personal friendship. In this Ben Hecht yarn, they respectively play Devlin, an American agent, and Alicia Huberman, the daughter of a convicted traitor, who join forces to ferret out Nazis in postwar Rio de Janeiro. But Claude Rains steals the acting honors as Alex Sebastian, the infatuated Nazi Alicia is forced to marry so that she can expose the enemy ring. What Devlin doesn't know is that Alicia has been found out by Alex and his clever, dominating mother (Mme. Leopoldine Konstantin), who set about slowly poisoning her. Devlin ultimately saves Alicia by brazening his way into the Sebastian home while Alex is entertaining suspicious colleagues, and carrying the ailing young lady out to a waiting car, leaving a frightened Alex behind on his doorstep. As the protagonists drive safely away, a figure in the doorway says, ominously, "Alex, we want to talk to you."

Among Hitchcock's finest thrillers, *Notorious* is replete with moments that remain indelibly in the viewer's memory: a long, surprisingly frank love scene between Devlin and Alicia in which a telephone call fails to interrupt their passionate kisses; Alex's scene with his mother in which he tells her the devastating truth he has just discovered ("Mother, I am married to an American spy."); Alicia's moment of drugged terror when she realizes that her coffee is poisoned, and many others. Best of all is the lavish party sequence— Hitchcock himself is glimpsed briefly at a punch bowl—with its famous tracking shot that descends from the top of a staircase to the crucial key to the wine cellar, clutched in Alicia's hand.

This scene is a model of Hitchcockian suspense. Devlin and Alicia slip away to investigate the wine cellar. She has removed the key from Alex's key

*NOTORIOUS (1946). With Ingrid Bergman.*

*NOTORIOUS (1946). With Claude Rains and Ingrid Bergman.*

ring, and a fast-dwindling supply of champagne informs us that, at any moment, someone will need the key to that wine cellar! Meanwhile, what the sleuthing pair discover—uranium particles in the wine bottles—sets the final plot-wheels in motion. In a moment of typical Hitchcock fright, Devlin and Alicia are discovered by Alex near the door of the wine cellar, but they quickly move into an embrace. Alex angrily reacts to what he thinks is a resumption of their previous affair. Or does he know better? Hitchcock doesn't tell us right away.

As Devlin, the Government agent torn between love and his job, Cary Grant gives a suave, solid performance that contrasts well with the vibrant beauty of Bergman in her prime. They are matched throughout by Rains, who is both sinister and touching as a mother-ridden man betrayed by the woman he adores. *Notorious* won Oscar nominations for Claude Rains and Ben Hecht's script, but received no awards.

Wisely continuing to appear in two pictures of his own selection per year, Grant entertained 1947 audiences with a pair of amusing RKO comedies, *The Bachelor and the Bobby-Soxer*, opposite Myrna Loy and Shirley Temple and, in a somewhat more whimsical vein, *The Bishop's Wife*.

Among the box-office winners of 1947 was *The Bachelor and the Bobby-Soxer*, a comedy that had an excellent cast, but a highly unlikely premise: audiences were asked to believe that Shirley Temple (then nineteen) and Myrna Loy (forty-five) could be sisters! Grant played a debonair, unattached man-about-town who finds he's the object of a schoolgirl infatuation. When the youngster (Temple) involves him in an innocently compromising situation, a lady judge (Loy), who happens to be the teenager's older sister, sentences him to escort the girl about until her crush wears off.

Sidney Sheldon's farcical screenplay evokes an atmosphere of delightful bewilderment that is well-served by its cast under the firm direction of Irving Reis. The fact that Sheldon won that year's Best Screenplay Oscar can be attributed as much to the polished light-comedy playing of an expert cast as to the basic material with which they worked. Certainly, Grant is in top form here, delivering all his self-patented mannerisms, whether cavorting in tux or casual clothing or indulging in a potato-sack race with Rudy Vallee and Johnny

*THE BACHELOR AND THE BOBBY-SOXER (1947). With Myrna Loy, Harry Davenport, Shirley Temple and Ray Collins.*

*THE BISHOP'S WIFE (1947). With Monty Woolley and Loretta Young.*

Sands. In a dream sequence, he even looks at home in a suit of shining armor.

*The Bishop's Wife*, produced by Samuel Goldwyn for RKO release, offers humor of a more gentle and disarming variety. Working from a novel by Robert Nathan, screenwriters Robert E. Sherwood and Leonardo Bercovici fashioned a sentimental and whimsical fable in which a debonair guardian angel named Dudley (Grant) comes down from heaven to lend spiritual comfort to Henry Brougham (David Niven), a young bishop in the middle of a church fund-raising crisis. Dudley's miraculous helping hand extends not only to the reluctant Henry, but also to his virtuous wife Julia (Loretta Young), in whom the visitor takes a slightly un-angelic interest.

Fantasy has never been among Hollywood's most successful commodities, but *The Bishop's Wife*, under the deft direction of Henry Koster (until then best known for his six Deanna Durbin films), brings it off in a delicate style that charmed 1947 yuletide moviegoers.

Cary Grant's beguiling performance as the heavenly helper belies the fact that he did not want to play the part and even, in the midst of production, of-

fered to return his salary, if he could be released from the picture. In this instance, the actor's wishes were overruled and the movie was completed. The result was a very pleasant film. In addition to Goldwyn's usual polished production values and the equally polished performances of its three stars, *The Bishop's Wife* boasts an exceptionally strong supporting cast which includes Monty Woolley (doing his joyful best to steal the picture), Elsa Lanchester (one of her eccentric gems), James Gleason, Gladys Cooper, Sara Haden, and Regis Toomey.

Despite his occasional critical successes in drama, it was clear that Cary Grant's public preferred him in light comedy. It was comedy that had put him among the screen's top money-makers, and in 1948 he did nothing to upset that status. Again, he teamed with Myrna Loy in David O. Selznick's enjoyable comedy of errors, *Mr. Blandings Builds His Dream House*, then costarred with a newcomer named Betsy Drake in a lesser effort entitled *Every Girl Should Be Married*.

*Mr. Blandings Builds His Dream House*, is a skillfully handled domestic farce about a New Yorker's mistaken notion of a home in Connecticut. Eric Hod-

*MR. BLANDINGS BUILDS HIS DREAM HOUSE (1948). With Myrna Loy and Melvyn Douglas.*

gins' droll novel laid the groundwork for an amusing screenplay by Norman Panama and Melvin Frank that used a series of inspired gags to underscore the less encouraging aspects of building the sort of rural retreat many an urban dweller thinks he wants. Peripherally, this story owes a debt to the George S. Kaufman-Moss Hart comedy, *George Washington Slept Here,* in which a Manhattan couple buy and attempt to restore a historic Pennsylvania house that's nearly falling down. In both cases, there are the unexpected problems with well-drilling, legal boundaries, local workmen, and outrageous price-gouging, to say nothing of hostile weather conditions and minor marital crises. In *Mr. Blandings Builds His Dream House,* the jokes are in expert hands for Grant, Loy, and Melvyn Douglas provide the innocent romantic triangle, while Reginald Denny, Tito Vuolo, Harry Shannon, and Ian Wolfe are among the canny Yankees out to take the Blandings for more than they're worth.

Cary Grant is at his most delightful as Jim Blandings, the impractical advertising executive whose city background hasn't prepared him to match wits with backwoods freebooters. Whether inadvertently tracking through a freshly-painted living room or getting locked in unfinished closets, his mounting frustrations are a pleasure to behold, and his reactions are timed to perfection. Amid the chaotic string of impossible mishaps that threaten to drive the Blandings and their children back to the skyscrapers forever, H.C. Potter, who had just directed Loretta Young's award-winning *The Farmer's Daughter*, wisely keeps the gags from getting out of hand. Indeed, it's the shock of recognition that enforces the success of much of the comedy in *Mr. Blandings Builds His Dream House*.

Late in 1947, while returning on the Queen Mary from a trip to England, Cary Grant was introduced by Merle Oberon to Betsy Drake, a young actress who had just scored a West End success in *Deep Are the Roots*, an American drama about racial problems in the modern South that had earlier won Broadway honors for Barbara Bel Geddes. Grant was impressed with Drake's charm, intelligence, and conversational skills and, when the voyage ended, he advised her to pursue her career on the West Coast. Subsequently, when she did so, Grant made a point of introducing her to Hollywood producers like Selznick and Dore Schary, and even got her a leading role in his next RKO film, *Every Girl Should Be Married*.

With a light sprinkling of

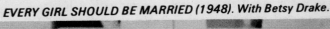

*EVERY GIRL SHOULD BE MARRIED (1948). With Betsy Drake.*

freshness and wit, screenwriters Don Hartman and Stephen Morehouse Avery offered a fairly bright comedy about the predatory pursuit of a marriageable baby specialist (Grant) by a disarmingly forthright and persevering young salesgirl (Drake), who employs grandiose schemes, her best friend (Diana Lynn), and a suave man-about-town (Franchot Tone) to land her prey. And, of course, she eventually gets her doctor.

Perhaps swayed by the good cheer of the 1948 Christmas season, the critics found this mediocre but diverting comedy rather pleasant, and they singled out Betsy Drake for special notice. This young actress's offbeat charm proved quite enchanting at times, but in so heavy an introductory dose as delivered here, under writer-producer Don Hartman's direction, it threatened to overwhelm both Grant and the picture. Possessed of an unusual speaking voice, Drake appeared to be aiming for an amalgam of the eccentric vocal and physical mannerisms of Margaret Sullavan and Katharine Hepburn. In some scenes, Cary Grant even plays on these mannerisms, allowing *his* character to mimic *her* affectations—displaying rather a curious treatment of his protegée, who appeared nonetheless unperturbed. *Every Girl Should Be Married* was the first of two movies in which he would costar with Betsy Drake—but his last appearance at RKO.

Having shared marquee billing with some of the best comedy actresses, Cary Grant now gained a costar so compatible that it is unfortunate they never teamed again. Howard Hawks' *I Was a Male War Bride* (released by Fox in 1949) cast him opposite Ann Sheridan, an actress who had progressed from small roles in Grant's mid-1930s Paramount comedies to prove herself as sensitive a dramatic actress (*Kings Row*) as she was adept at timing a clever line or wisecrack (*The Man Who Came to Dinner, The Doughgirls*).

I Was a Male War Bride gives screen credit to three writers—Charles Lederer, Leonard Spigelgass, and Hagar Wilde, who adapted the autobiographical novel by Henri Rochard. However, both Hawks and Sheridan have confirmed that much of the action and dialogue was ad-libbed and improvised as they filmed on location in Germany. Sheridan gives most of the credit to her costar: "The scene where we're in front of my commanding officer and she said, 'There's a hitch,' and he said 'Itch? Do you itch, Catherine?' And I said, 'No, I don't itch'—this was all Cary, all ad-lib. Howard Hawks would sit on the set and he'd say, 'Well, I'm not quite satisfied with this

scene. What would you say in a situation like this?' So we'd sit and think, and it was invariably Cary. He would tell you what to say. Howard is a very clever man. He picks brains. And he had a very clever brain to pick with Cary Grant, believe me. If only he had directed. I begged him. I said, 'Please get something and direct it before I'm too old to play comedy,' and he said, 'No, no dear, too much work. Not I. I want the drawing-room comedies—cigarette, anyone?'"

Much too attenuated and episodic, *I Was a Male War Bride* reflects the ten months that cast and crew spent making it—an uncommonly long production period, plagued by illness (Sheridan contracted pneumonia; Grant caught hepatitis) and the necessity of switching locations from Germany to England to Hollywood. Yet much of the comedy is inspired, as Henri Rochard, a romance-minded French Army officer (Grant) courts Lt. Catherine Gates (Sheridan), a WAC who's reluctant to get involved, due to past memories of their getting drunk together in a

111

*I WAS A MALE WAR BRIDE (1949). With Ann Sheridan.*

*I WAS A MALE WAR BRIDE (1949). With Ann Sheridan.*

wine cellar. The film's first half deals with Henri's embattled courtship of Catherine—he is sent off with her into the German countryside on a mission, bungles his assignment, and ends up in jail; in the last half, he marries Catherine, just as she's about to be shipped home, and battles red tape to be allowed to accompany her—a feat he accomplishes through that hoary old device of female impersonation, disguised as a WAC.

The movie's best scenes are those farcical moments that were undoubtedly devised on the spur of the moment: Grant forced to spend the night in the same room with an antagonistic Sheridan when their doorknob falls off—outside the door; Grant unaware that the motorcycle sidecar in which he is dozing has been set in motion by inquisitive children; Grant and Sheridan oblivious that the boat they're on is about to go over a waterfall; Grant in full WAC drag, exaggerating his own characteristic bowlegged walk, and sporting a frumpy wig made from a horse's tail. "Cary started out thinking it would be good if he acted rather effeminate," says Hawks. "We argued quite a bit, and I didn't seem to be winning. We were in Germany, and some general was giving a party, so I borrowed a

WAC's uniform and put on a red wig, with my legs, and Cary started to laugh right away. I went up to the general and got a cigar, and Cary came over to me and said, 'You can take those damn things off, because I'm sold.' The only thing he didn't quite like was making a wig out of a horse's tail."

In one of the film's funniest scenes, Grant climbs out a window to avoid being caught in Sheridan's room by the innkeeper's wife. He lands in an awning, which the unaware innkeeper then proceeds to wind up. As Grant thus rises into view in Sheridan's window, he quips, "I'm transparent. You can't even see me."

"I never could," she retorts, "not for sour apples," and she charges at him with a mop, sending him down into a haystack.

In *I Was a Male War Bride*, Grant employs all of his well-patented facial characteristics to great effect—the well-known distrustful look, the frequent deadpan face, and the ultra-serious expression with lowered brows and sidelong glances. And the familiar body movements suggesting that both his back and neck are confined by a metal brace.

Ann Sheridan has said that she and Grant wanted to do more films as a team with

Hawks, and that they often discussed the idea, "but there was just nothing that could come up to *Male War Bride*."

When, during filming, Grant came down with jaundice in London, Betsy Drake was constantly at his side. On Christmas Day of 1949, they were married in Phoenix, Arizona, in a simple ceremony in which Howard Hughes appeared as Cary's best man. The next morning, both newlyweds were back in Hollywood, making separate films.

The actor's only 1950 release, *Crisis*, again demonstrates Grant's willingness to entrust the direction of one of his movies to a novice—in this case, Richard Brooks, a highly respected screenwriter who had risen from the ridiculous but entertaining hokum of Maria Montez vehicles (*White Savage, Cobra Woman*) to forceful melodrama (*Brute Force, Key Largo*).

*Crisis*, made for MGM, concerns Dr. Eugene Ferguson (Grant), an American surgeon vacationing with his wife Helen (Paula Raymond) in a Latin American country on the verge of revolution. The plot hinges on Ferguson's being kidnapped to operate on the brain tumor of a dictator humorously named Farrago (Jose Ferrer). The operation, the doctor is informed bluntly, had better be successful. Brooks' screenplay made for an implausible but interesting melodrama which Grant plays with a dry, sardonic air, frequently characterized by a steely stare. A good supporting cast features Signe Hasso as the dictator's ruthless wife, Gilbert Roland as his mortal enemy who threatens to kill Helen if the operation saves Farrago, and former silent stars Ramon Novarro and Antonio Moreno in virtual bit roles.

Grant returned to Fox in 1951 to work, for the first and only time, under another leading writer-director, Joseph L. Mankiewicz. *People Will Talk*, a remake of a 1933 German film called *Dr. Praetorius*, is an adult and thoughtful, if highly verbose, comedy-drama that offers Grant as an unorthodox physician-teacher at odds with a meddling fellow-professor (Hume Cronyn) and in love with a pregnant student (Jeanne Crain), whom he marries. Professor accuses doctor of malpractice, which allows screenwriter Mankiewicz to discuss questions of medical ethics with wit, intelligence, and humor. The most entertaining of these discussions are between the doctor and his friend, an atomic scientist and occasional bull-fiddle player (Walter Slezak).

*CRISIS (1950). With Signe Hasso, Jose Ferrer, Antonio Moreno and Mario Siletti.*

*PEOPLE WILL TALK (1951). With Sidney Blackmer and Jeanne Crain.*

In *The New York Times*, Bosley Crowther called *People Will Talk*, "vastly entertaining," singling out the acting of Cronyn and Grant, whose performance he called, "an effective mixture of medicine and merriment." But for audiences conditioned to the brilliant flair for humor and the ability to capture human foibles displayed by Mankiewicz in *All About Eve* and *A Letter to Three Wives*, *People Will Talk* left something to be desired.

Cary Grant's two 1952 comedies range from the pleasantly minor *(Room for One More)* to the occasionally inspired *(Monkey Business)*. In the former, he again appeared opposite Betsy Drake in a Warners film that is now shown on television as *The Easy Way*, to avoid confusion with syndicated reruns of a short-lived 1962 comedy series (also called *Room for One More*) that came from the same source, a book by Anna Perrott Rose. This true story about a couple who open their home to needy children had a Melville Shavelson-Jack Rose script that drew its humor from the expected complications that arise in a house full of children and animals. Norman Taurog, a comedy veteran since the early days of talkies, directed this heartwarming, family-oriented mixture for

its full quota of sentiment and laughs, but ultimately allowed the story's more mawkish aspects to undermine the proceedings.

Again, Drake and Grant make a good comedy team, when not being upstaged by the scene-stealing youngsters and livestock. Grant's vexed reactions to the birth of kittens under his stove is an amusing highlight, and his efforts to have a romantic interlude with his wife, despite the interruptions of small fry, provide a measure of fun—but not enough.

Howard Hawks' *Monkey Business*, made for Fox in 1952, marks Grant's fifth and last film with that director. This throwback to the old days of "screwball" farce supports a fanciful premise that demands a lot of suspended disbelief from its audience. A scatterbrained screenplay by the team of I.A.L. Diamond, Charles Lederer, and Ben Hecht had Cary Grant as an absentminded, bespectacled professor named Barnaby Fulton, whose chief preoccupation is the discovery of a drug that will rejuvenate. (He's called it B-4, so that they can promote it as "B-4 and after.") Before Barnaby thinks he has his product properly mixed, a laboratory chimpanzee gets loose, unknowingly happens to complete the formula and pours it into the lab's supply

*ROOM FOR ONE MORE (1952). With Betsy Drake, Iris Mann, George Winslow, Malcolm Cassell, Gay Gordon and Clifford Tatum Jr.*

*MONKEY BUSINESS (1952). With Ginger Rogers, Jerry Sheldon and Marilyn Monroe.*

of drinking water, with the result that Barnaby and his wife, Edwina (Ginger Rogers) revert to teenagers and a complete reversal of normal behavior patterns.

With the basic idea established, writers, director, and cast indulge in whacky situations that generate a lot of laughter but wear a bit thin before the ninety-seven minutes are over. But a willing cast, including Charles Coburn, Marilyn Monroe (as a purely decorative secretary named Lois Laurel), Hugh Marlowe, and Larry Keating, threw themselves into the proceedings with obvious dedication and a complete abandon to the nonsensical. Here, Cary Grant, his eyeglasses discarded and his hair reduced to a crew-cut, wears wildly youthful clothing and whizzes about town in a sports car. Among the actor's best moments are those in which he recognizes the legs of Monroe as she walks behind a billboard, and the lab scenes in which he battles to upstage a scene-stealing monkey. When nearly everyone has taken a sip from the "doctored" water cooler, chaos erupts predictably, with a sequence involving actors and chimp in an orgy of seltzer-spraying.

Hawks says, "I don't believe the premise of *Monkey Business* was really believable, and for that reason the film was not as funny as it should have been. The laughs are born out of the inhibitions that restrict each of us and are here abruptly removed by rejuvenation. It was a good story. Perhaps we pushed the point a bit too far for the public."

Cary Grant has reportedly had misgivings about certain roles once filming was underway. He has also, on occasion, indulged in last-minute changes of mind about roles he had already agreed to play. During this period, he turned down leading parts in two Audrey Hepburn pictures, *Roman Holiday* and *Sabrina*, and was replaced, respectively, by Gregory Peck and Humphrey Bogart. He might also have starred opposite Judy Garland in George Cukor's remake of *A Star is Born*, had he not had second thoughts. Instead of these worthwhile roles, Grant elected to appear opposite Deborah Kerr in an old-fashioned romantic comedy entitled *Dream Wife* at MGM. In this slight concoction of writers Sidney Sheldon, Herbert Baker, and Alfred Lewis Levitt, with Sheldon directing, Grant is an urbane American male who jilts his career-girl fiancée (Kerr) to wed an Eastern princess (Betta St.

*DREAM WIFE (1953). With Deborah Kerr.*

John), who has been trained to satisfy every whim of the man she marries. Much of the movie's humor derives from the differences between Eastern and American customs. Both Grant and Kerr are in top comedy form, are beautifully photographed and at their most attractive. However, Grant's box-office power had been waning for some time and MGM, which had filmed this lavishly set and costumed comedy in black and white, released the film with a minimal publicity campaign in mid-summer of 1953. Later that year, the actor decided to retire. His explanation: "It was the period of the blue jeans, the dope addicts, the Method, and nobody cared about comedy at all."

Over two years passed before another Cary Grant film appeared on the screen. Alfred Hitchcock was the one responsible, not only for changing Grant's mind about retirement, but also for rejuvenating his career. Grant had kept in top shape, did not *want* to stay retired, and he liked the screenplay for *To Catch a Thief*. Also tempting was the prospect of Grace Kelly, then Hitchcock's favorite leading lady, as his costar, and French Riviera locations.

In this handsomely produced light-comedy thriller, Grant plays John Robie, a smooth, retired cat burglar who, to clear his own reputation, helps track down a jewel thief who is imitating Robie's methods, while defying the bumbling Riviera gendarmes. Cleverly intertwined is Robie's sophisticated romance with Frances Stevens (Grace Kelly), a coolly beautiful American husband-hunter traveling with her vulgar, diamond-encrusted mother (Jessie Royce Landis). During the course of this tricky John Michael Hayes script, nearly everyone in sight, at one time or another, comes under suspicion, before the exciting denouement that takes place at night during a lavish costume party, with Robie cornering the real thief on a treacherous villa

# HITCHCOCK LURES HIM BACK

rooftop.

With tongue firmly tucked in his cheek, Hitchcock stirs this highly entertaining brew with potent dashes of sex (Kelly's cold beauty soon proves a deceptive cover-up for a highly sexual nature hovering just beneath the ice) and *double-entendre* dialogue (Serving chicken to Grant, Kelly inquires, "Will you have a breast or a leg?"). The Cote d'Azur had never been more bountifully served by the camera, and Robert Burks won an Oscar for his color photography.

For the movie's suspenseful final scenes, Cary Grant had to sublimate his natural acrophobia and scamper, without benefit of a safety net, over some steeply tiled location rooftops. That he did so without letting his actual terror show is a tribute to his professionalism. In *To Catch a Thief*, Hitchcock makes his customary "cameo" appearance in a bus sequence, where he's discovered sitting next to Grant. The film received excellent notices and was a popular moneymaker when Paramount released it during the summer of 1955.

Grant calls himself "a quivering mass of indecision," and admits that it was his own fault that he didn't play the William Holden role in *The Bridge on the River Kwai*. He had read the book, and the film's producer, Sam Spiegel, had approached him for it. Grant was interested, but admits he hemmed and hawed too much over script changes and the fact that the film meant going to Ceylon on location—a prospect that discouraged him, since he and Betsy had been doing a lot of traveling. "Meanwhile," says the actor, "Columbia, knowing me, had also sent a script to Bill Holden. Holden read the story, decided it was magnificent, which it was, and said he'd do it. By then, of course, I realized what a great part I had lost."

Following the Hitchcock movie, no other scripts interested Cary Grant, and again he was off the screen for nearly two years. The film he selected for his next comeback was ill-advised. Stanley Kramer's *The Pride and the Passion* (1957), filmed in Spain for United Artists release, is a costume adventure loosely adapt-

*TO CATCH A THIEF (1955). With Grace Kelly.*

ed from C.S. Forester's short novel "The Gun" by the writing team of Edna and Edward Anhalt. It was a costly, large-scale production with three expensive stars (Grant, Sophia Loren, Frank Sinatra) and a giant cannon, which gets dragged about the Spanish countryside in 1810, as guerilla resistance fighters carry on a losing battle against Napoleon's conquering forces in the mountains. Grant played Capt. Anthony Trumbull, the British ordnance expert who goes to Spain to engineer getting the cannon out of a mountain ravine, where it has been abandoned by Spanish troops. Ultimately, the big gun is hauled to the walls of Avila, where a bloody siege is fought. Sinatra was colorful, if rather improbable, as Miguel, the Spanish peasant leader who dies for his cause. Loren played Juana, Sinatra's woman who finds herself torn between him and Grant. In the end, she too dies.

*The Pride and the Passion* received a tremendous drubbing by the critics, who thought Cary Grant and his fellow players were largely upstaged by that cannon in a film as overblown and static as it was long (132 minutes).

*TO CATCH A THIEF (1955). As John Robie.*

122

Clearly, Grant was out of his element here, and actually appeared, at times, disinterested. As for producer Kramer's direction, critical praise was reserved largely for his action scenes. The film was not a success.

During production of the Kramer film, there were reports of a romance between Grant and his married costar, Sophia Loren, with whom he wanted to re-team in an American-made film. Instead, she returned to Italy and her most important dramatic role in Vittorio de Sica's *Two Women*. Meanwhile, Betsy Drake, who had visited her husband on location, returned to the U.S. by ship. On the night of July 25, 1956, she was a passenger on the ill-fated *Andrea Doria* when it collided with the *Stockholm* off Nantucket Island, with a loss of fifty-one lives. As soon as *The Pride and the Passion* was finished, Grant flew to her in New York, where their subsequent reunion helped to reinforce their marriage, as well as to quiet the gossip columnists.

Leo McCarey's sentimental romantic drama, *Love Affair*, had provided one of the highlights of 1939 filmgoing, for critics and audiences alike. Its past popularity motivated McCarey to film a 1957 remake, which he retitled *An Affair to Remember*.

**THE PRIDE AND THE PASSION (1957). With Sophia Loren.**

This time, Cary Grant and Deborah Kerr were the lovers so movingly portrayed in the earlier film by Charles Boyer and Irene Dunne. Though much inferior to the original version, this glossy soap opera, about a couple who share a shipboard romance and decide to let six months pass before meeting again (only to be separated further by a tragic accident), proved immensely popular with the public. The script, on which McCarey and Delmer Daves made some revisions, was most entertaining in the earlier

123

*AN AFFAIR TO REMEMBER (1957). With Deborah Kerr.*

shipboard scenes, when Grant (at his most ruefully charming) and Kerr were required to be merely witty and sophisticated. Symptomatic of the film's problems was the fact that Eastman Color and CinemaScope had now been added to a little black and white movie that had run some eighty-seven minutes eighteen years earlier. *An Affair to Remember* is 115 minutes long.

Talking about this film's production, Deborah Kerr illuminates the "murderous" problems inherent in seemingly smooth scenes of lovemaking: "Cary and I danced a few turns, gave each other tender glances, alternated singing a line or two. We had to dance cheek-to-cheek, slowly, dreamily; separate while one or the other sang; remember to turn so that Cary's face would be in the camera when he sang or spoke and vice versa; remembering that both of our faces had to be in camera range for reaction shots." And she concludes, "I'd much sooner learn ten pages of dialogue, and I know Cary would, too!"

With *Kiss Them for Me*, Cary Grant joined forces with producer-director Stanley Donen (with whom he would make four pictures) to form Grandon Productions. Fox released this comedy, adapted by Julius Epstein from both the short-lived Luther Davis play of the same name and the play's source, Frederic Wakeman's excellent novel, *Shore Leave*. This tale about three Navy fliers on leave in San Francisco had an occasionally disarming air of tough, cynical humor, well handled by Grant, Ray Walston, and Larry Blyden. The picture was less well served by its female headliners: ex-model Suzy Parker, lovely but stiff in her screen debut; and the buxom, grotesque Jayne Mansfield, whose bleached-blonde vulgarity ("Is your hair natural?" "Yes, except for the color.") did not blend well with the Grant style. Donen's direction of this familiar material was very uneven.

Much has been made of Cary Grant's use of the drug LSD. Actually, it involved a period of psychiatric experiment during which the actor, with his wife's encouragement, underwent carefully doctor-controlled treatments. As Grant later explained, "What LSD does is release the mind to a fantastic degree. You have waking dreams, and sometimes weird and wonderful hallucinations. But, most important, it cuts down psychoanalysis to a very short period. For anyone like me, who has a deep-rooted desire for understanding and peace of mind, it's almost like a miracle."

As a result of these sessions, Cary Grant was noticeably more open with interviewers and columnists, and he took a more active interest in his mother, who still lived in Bristol in her late eighties. It also precipitated a formal separation from Betsy Drake, with the announcement that, although there were no divorce plans, their marriage had not brought the happiness both desired, and so they had decided to "separate for awhile." But

*KISS THEM FOR ME (1957).* **With Jack Mullaney and Jayne Mansfield.**

they continued to share occasional dates with one another, and Grant always spent Betsy's birthday with her, even if it meant a flight to or from Europe.

Audience response to *Indiscreet,* Grant's next film, was far more favorable than to *Kiss Them for Me.* His choice of Ingrid Bergman as a costar may have had a lot to do with it. Based on Norman Krasna's frothy play, *Kind Sir,* a featherweight item that had survived on Broadway largely through the collective personal charm of

*INDISCREET (1958). With Ingrid Bergman.*

Charles Boyer and Mary Martin, *Indiscreet* had a screenplay which Krasna had revised and improved. It also had two charismatic stars at their brightest, sporting handsome wardrobes and cavorting on lavish sets. Again, this was a Grandon Production, with Stanley Donen directing for Warner Brothers release. The result had scant substance—the film amounts to very little—but Bergman and Grant play delightfully together and make their audiences think they've seen a much better film than is actually there. And so this slight Lubitsch-like soufflé about the middle-aged romance of a marriage-shy financial expert and a successful actress was very popular with the public. Among the film's comic highlights was a fancy officers' ball at which a straight-faced Grant unexpectedly broke into a variation on the Highland fling. "I got a real kick out of dancing again," said Grant. "I also wound up with a fantastic charley horse."

*Houseboat* (1958) took the fifty-three-year-old Grant back to Paramount for another teaming with Sophia Loren, this time with subject matter far removed from *The Pride and the Passion*. This Melville Shavelson-Jack Rose family comedy offered Grant as a wealthy Washington attorney whose estranged wife's death leaves him in charge of three young children. Loren was the rebellious daughter of a visiting Italian symphony conductor who is mistaken by Grant for a slightly trampish domestic when she brings home his runaway younger son. Because of her knack with children, he then hires her as a maid, and they take up residence on a Potomac River houseboat, because of a housing shortage. Inevitably, romance takes over, with Grant and Loren involved not only with one another, but also, respectively, with Martha Hyer and Harry Guardino, prior to the predictable Grant-Loren finale.

The critics seemed united in praising *Houseboat*'s three child-actors, Charles Herbert, Mimi Gibson, and Paul Petersen, but were divided over how much taste (or lack of it) was contained in a script that used sexual innuendo so frequently (but, nevertheless, received an Oscar nomination). However, many found the movie entertaining, and were pleased by the adult performances and the picturesque views of Washington, D.C., where many scenes were shot. The film was a very popular one, and Sophia Loren reported she had learned more from working with Grant than with any previous fellow-player.

Alfred Hitchcock says he sought Cary Grant for the role of the pursued and harassed hero of his classic 1959 thriller *North By Northwest*, because "audiences can identify with him." In this film, the hero is almost never offscreen, so the star gets quite a workout.

*North By Northwest* is an original Ernest Lehman script that weaves a richly complex suspense tale of spies and mistaken identity—a tangled skein of exciting events and improbable

*HOUSEBOAT (1958). With Mimi Gibson, Charles Herbert and Sophia Loren.*

plot turns that amuses and entertains nonstop for 136 minutes. All of the action centers on Grant as Roger O. Thornhill, an innocent advertising executive who is kidnapped by gunmen from New York's Plaza Hotel, hustled off to a Long Island estate, framed for murder at the United Nations building, and forced to flee to Chicago on the 20th Century Limited, where he meets Eve Kendall (Eva Marie Saint), a sophisticated blonde who offers to help him. Later, Thornhill barely survives a strafing attack by a crop-dusting plane at a deserted prairie crossroads, only to learn that Eve is the mistress of his would-be killer, Phillip Vandamm (James Mason). The finale is one of Hitchcock's characteristic best—Eve and Thornhill flee murderous spies across the giant stone faces of the Mount Rushmore memorial.

Filmed for MGM in 1959, *North By Northwest*, with *Psycho* and *The Birds*, stands among the very best of Hitchcock's later thrillers. Lehman's screenplay, for which he justly won an Academy Award nomination, is a masterpiece of sly humor and delicious ambiguity. The audience is never permitted to know just what all the fuss is about (except a vague reference to "government secrets"), or why so many people's lives are at stake. Obviously, it's not all that important. Hitchcock himself has referred to the film as "pure fantasy," terming it his "American *39 Steps*."

*North By Northwest* contains scenes that are surely among many filmgoers' favorites, whether it's the unexpected, sudden attack on Grant by the swooping byplane whose "crop dust" is bullets, or Grant's "assassination" by a deliberately blank-firing Eva Marie Saint in a crowded restaurant. There are others: the literal cliff-hanging climax up and down the (studio-built) images of Washington, Lincoln, Jefferson, and Teddy Roosevelt; or the unforgettable elevator scene in which Thornhill and his mother (Jessie Royce Landis) are crowded in with two of his would-be assassins. When

*NORTH BY NORTHWEST (1959). With Eva Marie Saint, James Mason and Martin Landau.*

*NORTH BY NORTHWEST (1959). With Eva Marie Saint.*

he tries to communicate this fact to her, she smilingly accosts the villains with, "You gentlemen aren't *really* trying to kill my son, are you?" In a moment, everyone on the crowded elevator is laughing—except the glowering Thornhill. Also remembered is the amusingly suggestive repartee between Grant and Saint on a night train to Chicago. Hitchcock himself calls the movie "one big joke," and admits that he filmed this story with tongue in cheek. Typical of his sly sense of humor, he adds, "When Cary Grant was on Mount Rushmore, I would have liked to put him into Lincoln's nostril and let him have a sneezing fit." Incidentally, though obvious fakes, the Mount Rushmore stone faces were constructed in such depth that they required hero and heroine to work high above one of Hollywood's tallest sound stages, and Grant insists this is the picture that finally conquered his acrophobia. *North By Northwest* delighted film reviewers and proved a tremendous financial success for MGM.

Grant's only other 1959 movie, *Operation Petticoat*, is a significant landmark in that it began a very successful association for him with Universal in

*OPERATION PETTICOAT (1959). With Joan O'Brien.*

*THE GRASS IS GREENER (1960). With Deborah Kerr, Robert Mitchum and Jean Simmons.*

popular films on which he was usually at least an associate producer. Consequently, most of the picture's profits went to him, thus swelling the coffers of a star who was already several times a millionaire. Like many of his later films, this Granart (Cary Grant-Robert Arthur) production utilized a scriptwriting team (Stanley Shapiro-Maurice Richlin) that won an Oscar nomination for its efforts, while director Blake Edwards handled the proceedings in a manner that Paul V. Beckley of the *New York Herald-Tribune* called, "direct, uncluttered, and sensitive to comic balance."

*Operation Petticoat* is merely fanciful World War II service nonsense about a co-ed submarine in the Pacific islands that gets painted pink due to a supply shortage. Cary Grant's costar this time was Tony Curtis, who was here allowed to express his adulation of Grant by performing in a role and accent that seemed to mimic the older star, if somewhat less so than his brilliant Grant impersonation in *Some Like It Hot,* earlier that year. Released for the 1959 Christmas trade, *Operation Petticoat* was a huge success at the box office.

Grant then turned down an offer from his old friend, director George Cukor, to play opposite Marilyn Monroe in *Let's Make Love,* as did Yul Brynner, Gregory Peck, Charlton Heston, Rock Hudson, and James Stewart. Perhaps they were all wary of coping with that lady's well-known peccadilloes. For this film, French star Yves Montand proved less resistant.

In 1960, Grant again teamed with director Stanley Donen on their Grandon production of *The Grass is Greener,* filmed in England from an adaptation by Hugh and Margaret Williams of their stage play. The film had an attractive quartet of stars in Grant, Deborah Kerr, Robert Mitchum, and Jean Simmons and, though strong on charm, was too lightweight and frothy for most critics. Nor did audiences support it to the degree that had been anticipated.

The plot had Grant and Kerr portraying impoverished British landed gentry who decide to open their home to paying tourists. Mitchum is the American oil millionaire who falls for Kerr (and she for him), thus precipitating an amusing marital mix-up compounded by the presence of a giddy madcap, delightfully played by Jean Simmons, who blithely stole every scene in which she appeared.

The plays of Hugh and Margaret Williams, more successful on British than American stages, depend largely on a dexterous use of the English language and a satirical style of performance akin to the plays of Noel Coward. When not competing with Simmons' deliciously larcenous performance, the film's three other stars deliver their light-comedy beautifully. Grant, in particular, is in very good form, especially in scenes with an unusual butler, played to perfection by Moray Watson. *Time* magazine's critic thought little of *The Grass is Greener*, but took an opportunity to appraise the Cary Grant style:

"Actor Grant, as usual, is the mainstay of the show. He is the only funnyman in movie history who has maintained himself for close to thirty years as a ranking romantic star. He wears only one expression: the bland mask of drawing-room comedy. He plays only one part: the well-pressed, elegantly laundered masculine existence that suddenly finds itself splashed by love's old sweet ketchup. About that situation Grant has nothing important to say, no social or moral message to deliver. He creates in a vacuum of values; he is a technician only—but he is a technician of genius."°

°*Time* (Jan. 6, 1961).

**THAT TOUCH OF MINK (1962).**
**With Doris Day.**

Cary Grant next teamed his own production company (now named "Granley") with two others: writer-producer Stanley Shapiro's Nob Hill Corporation and Arwin, the organization owned by Martin Melcher and his wife Doris Day, with whom Grant would costar. Their vehicle: *That Touch of Mink*, a comedy written by Shapiro and Nate Monaster, about a bachelor business-executive (Grant) trying to compromise an honest working girl (Day) on a trip to Bermuda. In short, it's the old Doris Day formula involving a virtuous, if mature, female, fighting to maintain her virginity through all sorts of titillating situations, rife with innuendo. In the end, of course, girl gets boy to marry her, thus upholding her reputation at all costs.

Delbert Mann, whose previous credits included the Oscar-winning *Marty* and *Separate Tables*, as well as the Doris Day-Rock Hudson *Lover Come Back*, directed with a bright eye for pace and well-timed visual humor. Grant and Day made a good comedy team, although the actress got most of the laughs with some highly skilled clowning. (In one of their best scenes together, he finds her drunk in the bedroom, with an empty scotch bottle stuck on her big toe.) Released by Universal-International in the early summer of 1962, *That Touch of Mink* proved another popular money-maker for its stars—and again drew Oscar nominations for the screenwriters Cary Grant had been wise enough to hire.

Grant then lost out on a role that he wanted very much to play—Henry Higgins in the screen version of *My Fair Lady*. Despite Rex Harrison's immense success in this part, it is interesting to speculate how effective Grant might have been, especially with his ability to sing.

That summer, the actor's over-twelve-year marriage to Betsy Drake—his longest—came to an end when she obtained a divorce on August 13th, on the grounds of mental cruelty. "He appeared to be bored with me," she reported. "He once told me he didn't want to be married. He showed no interest in any of my friends." Later, she told the press, "I was always in love with him—and still am." Cary Grant had no retort, no unkind words for Betsy. Supposedly, they have remained on good terms. About this time, Grant became interested in Camille Diane Friesen, a starlet some thirty-four years his junior, who was ambitiously forging an acting career under the name of Dyan Cannon. Before flying to Paris to costar with Audrey Hepburn in *Charade*, Grant travelled to Philadelphia, where Dyan was featured with Jane Fonda, Bradford Dillman, and Ben Piazza in the tryout of a play called *The Fun Couple* which lasted for three performances on Broadway.

Stanley Donen's *Charade* (1963) owes a great deal to the Hitchcock school of intrigue and

*CHARADE (1963). With James Coburn.*

suspense, offering handsome stars (Grant and the Givenchy-gowned Audrey Hepburn) in an amusing and entertaining melodrama set against handsome backgrounds (mostly Paris, beautifully photographed by Charles Lang, Jr.). Hepburn played the freshly-widowed Reggie Lambert, whose estranged husband's murder uncovers the fact that he was in possession of an unaccounted-for $250,000, now being sought by his three mayhem-minded ex-OSS buddies (George Kennedy, James Coburn, Ned Glass). Grant was Peter Joshua, a mystery man who comes to the young widow's aid when her life is threatened by the gang. Peter

Stone's screenplay is rife with clever, implausible plot twists, and of course Joshua is not what he seems. Is he trying to help Reggie? Or does he want to kill her? It would be unfair to prospective viewers to reveal the aftermath of the movie's thrilling chase climax.

*Charade* is top-notch entertainment, wrapped in as glittering a package of fun and games as moviegoers had witnessed since *North By Northwest.* Despite a wide age difference, Audrey Hepburn (thirty-four) and the graying but physically-fit Grant (fifty-nine, but looking forty-five) make an excellent team, completely plausible even

*CHARADE (1963). With Audrey Hepburn.*

in their witty romantic scenes. Sensibly, Stanley Donen directs this confusing but stylish movie at a rapid pace, diluting the more violent moments with humor, and always maintaining an eye for the visual. And the proceedings are neatly underscored by Henry Mancini's brittle music.

Director Howard Hawks then tried, without success, to get Grant and Audrey Hepburn for his comedy, *Man's Favorite Sport?*, but settled for Rock Hudson and Paula Prentiss. The film was not a landmark.

Ralph Nelson's *Father*

*Goose*, a 1964 Granox (Grant) production for Universal release, ostensibly offered the public a radically different Cary Grant. Publicity releases offered alarming reports of an unkempt, unshaven, and grubby-looking character actor who might still be recognizable as the once-suave sophisticate known as Cary Grant. Yet the Cary Grant who starred in the Christmas feature at New York's Radio City Music Hall maintained enough of the old Grant image to allay the fears of his fans. The actor's hair was now thoroughly gray, his wardrobe was that of a casual Pacific islands beachcomber, and his well-tanned face bore the stubble of a couple of days' growth, but his surface grubbiness could hardly hide the sardonic Grant wit, the age-defying energy or the flair for scenes of frantic farce.

*Father Goose* relates a thin story about Walter Eckland, a cantankerous boozer who's pressed into service during World War II to man a strategic South Seas watching station. Into this sanctuary intrudes Catherine Freneau (Leslie Caron), a prim Frenchwoman in charge of seven schoolgirls, marooned enroute from New Zealand to New Guinea. The inevitable romance takes a long time to get going. Before that, there are some amusing exchanges between Walter and Catherine. As he guzzles his scotch, she interjects with an eye to the girls, "Mr. Eckland, must you?" To which he retorts, "What are you—some kind of religious fanatic?" Or, once they've invaded his humble hut, she inquires, "Mr. Eckland, where are the tea things?" "Last time I looked," he replies drily, "they were next to the finger bowls!"

This flimsy collaboration of no less than three writers (S.H. Barnett, Peter Stone, and Frank Tarloff) spends too much time on small jokes before moving on to the emergency-operation scene in which Catherine mistakenly thinks she's been bitten by a poisonous snake and Walter has to minister to her, sucking the "venom" from her wounded leg, while she becomes drunk from his scotch, to kill the pain. Tipsily, she asks him, "What did my blood taste like?" And he comes back with, "How would I know? I'm not a vampire."

At times, the story gets self-consciously "cute," as when one of the more nubile schoolgirls plays up to Walter, and he makes a phony pass at her with "What time shall I expect you tonight?" —which sends the child scurrying away in a fright. The film grows tiresome before a climax that offers some excitement when the island is strafed by a Japanese plane. And, somehow, when Walter wins Catherine at the film's end, it defies audience belief. If Cary Grant seems to have lost his old romantic touch, then perhaps the combination of screenplay, setting, wardrobe, director, and costar offered odds against which even *he* couldn't compete.

Grant selected Leslie Caron to play opposite him in that film, "because she is a relaxed performer, one of the few perfectly relaxed actresses on the screen."

*FATHER GOOSE (1964).* With Leslie Caron.

At the time, he also disclosed some facts about his functions as an actor-producer: "I am the producer—the executive producer—but I hire a producer. I get the best director I can find. I obtain the services of an excellent scriptwriter and request his presence on the set in order to be on the scene if changes-for-the-better are necessary. I work along with a film editor, but I have the last word on the editing. Naturally, I choose the story and the cast. And I have no financial problems—Universal furnishes the money."*

*Father Goose* proved another successful movie for Grant, and when screenwriter Peter Stone accepted an Oscar for his work on that film, he said, "My thanks to Cary Grant, who keeps winning these things for other people."

No Grant films followed in 1965. His big event that year was his secret July 22 marriage in Las

*The Daily News, interview by Wanda Hale. (Dec. 7, 1964.)

Vegas to Dyan Cannon. Eleven days went by before the press discovered the news. By then, the honeymooners had gone to England, where the actor introduced his bride to his aged mother. Soon afterwards, Grant went to Tokyo for location scenes on *Walk, Don't Run*, a reasonably amusing comedy that, at this writing, appears to be his swan song. That October 14, while the star was still in Japan, reports were confirmed that, at sixty-two Cary Grant would become a father for the first time—the following May.

Under the Granley banner, Grant had hired Sol C. Siegel to produce *Walk, Don't Run* for Columbia Pictures. With its details altered and its plot updated, this Sol Saks screenplay was nothing more than a remake of *The More the Merrier*, one of the brightest films of 1943. And, in the roles so superbly played for director George Stevens by Charles Coburn, Jean Arthur, and Joel McCrea—were Grant, Samantha Eggar, and Jim Hutton. Whereas the earlier comedy had centered on Washington's wartime housing shortage—a situation that evoked many laughs in more than one film—*Walk, Don't Run* now dealt with a similar housing shortage in Tokyo during the 1964 Olympics. The idea is a good one, and Charles

*WALK, DON'T RUN (1966). With Jim Hutton.*

*WALK, DON'T RUN (1966). With Samantha Eggar.*

Walters' direction helped his attractive cast go through the amusing situations with style and grace. For those unfamiliar with *The More the Merrier*, the fun is considerable; for those with memories, the movie is a sorry second-best—like comparing MGM's 1956 *High Society* to its derivative, *The Philadelphia Story*.

For once, in *Walk, Don't Run*, Cary Grant doesn't get the girl. He is strictly on the scene to act as Cupid (albeit a suave and sartorially elegant Cupid, who still has an eye for female beauty —and a family back home in Britain), and even manages to join a walking-race in his underwear, in order to get to competing athlete Hutton and help him smooth out his romantic problems with Eggar. Much of the film's fun focused on the problems of apartment-sharing, matching time-tables, working out bathroom arrangements, etc. Aside from running in the Olympics, the story even had Grant clambering around on a Japanese rooftop and getting shut out of his room.

In this film, the famous Grant voice often sounds husky and gravelly. But his sardonic wit and timing are still very much in evidence. At the film's start, a prissy embassy clerk says to him, "Sir William, may I say what a pleasure it is to meet you in person." To which Grant replies curtly, "Only if you *must!*"

After Eggar allows Grant to share her Tokyo flat, she asks him, "Are you married?" "Yes," he answers, "why?" "Well, I think you might have told me," she counters. To which he quips, "Why? What did you have in mind?" Perhaps the old romantic Cary Grant image was one screenwriter Saks couldn't resist. Or—better still—perhaps it was one Grant *himself* couldn't resist. . . .

*Walk, Don't Run* opened to excellent reviews in the summer of 1966, and the public flocked to it. *Variety* thought Grant was "at the peak of his comedy prowess." In *The New York Times*, Howard Thompson wrote, "It is the genial, suave sportsmanship of the veteran star, as the spry, gray-domed Cupid that prods *Walk, Don't Run* into such a disarming trot. Yesterday, Grant took Tokyo."

The actor's firstborn was expected to arrive in May of 1966. Instead, she was born prematurely, weighing in at a healthy four pounds, eight ounces, on February 26, 1966. They named her Jennifer. At sixty-two, Cary Grant was ecstatic about his new role, and he spoke candidly to the press: "I've waited all my life hoping for children, and when you've waited for such a long time, you hope like mad that everything will work out all right. In my case, I knew the birth of my baby was the chance of a dream coming true. It's never too late to become a parent."

As to his professional plans, Grant then admitted that romantic leads were behind him, and he added, "By now, my choice of subjects is very limited, I may wind up playing some old retired banker in a wheel chair. I want to go on and on, like Sir C. Aubrey Smith." He also remarked that he had no plans, and that *Walk, Don't Run* might be his last film. "I find the economics of this business very exciting," he said, "because of the great sums involved. It's what I can do happiest. It's a profession, like any other. If I knew of a better one, I'd do it."

Grant's May-December marriage to Dyan Cannon did not last out the year. On December 28, 1966, it was announced that they had separated. He tried to effect a reconciliation; she refused and, on August 22, 1967, in Los Angeles Superior Court, Dyan sued Cary for divorce, charging "cruel and inhuman" treatment.

At that time, it was estimated that Cary Grant was worth "more than $10 million," with a yearly income in excess of $500,000. Dyan demanded "reasonable support" for herself and Jennifer, with her monthly expenses estimated at $5,470. Grant was not expected to contest her suit, but he did, with considerable "dirty linen" aired before the final outcome; Dyan would receive fifty thousand dollars a year in alimony and child support, and Grant was permitted two months annual visitation rights. Later, this was amended, and Grant has been able to spend a great deal of time with Jennifer, whom he adores. Also, he and Dyan have managed to

*Receiving his Oscar from Frank Sinatra (1970).*

settle past differences, for the sake of their child. And, although his relationship with her is not on a par with his lasting friendships with Barbara Hutton and Betsy Drake, Cary Grant and Dyan Cannon have remained cordial.

Soon thereafter, the actor entered the beauty business, when he became a board member for Rayette-Fabergé. Although he didn't need the money, his new salary was a mere drop in the bucket, compared with the one million dollars (plus percentage of the profits) he had been making on his more recent films. He was now paid a salary of fifteen thousand dollars a year, plus two hundred dollars for each directors' meeting he attended and "eventual stock options."

As for his film career, Grant told reporters in 1969, "I'm not really making pictures and I don't know whether I'll ever make any—or whether I'll make one or ten." The following year, he made an unbilled "guest appearance" in MGM's *Elvis— That's the Way It Is,* an interesting documentary covering an Elvis Presley concert in Las Vegas. Grant was one of several celebrities interviewed on his way in to that concert. In the spring of 1973, aged sixty-nine, he admitted to a *Variety* reporter that he had no intention of returning to moviemaking. "I've had it," he said. "I can't think of going back and listening to all that deplorable conversation on the set, and go tripping over all those cables." In fact, he much prefers devoting his time to traveling for Rayette-Fabergé, and devoting his energies to his daughter. "Jennifer is my life today," he has said. "I plan around her, where she is, when I may have her."

For a movie star of his stature, personality, and talent, it is a shameful Hollywood oversight that Cary Grant has never received an Academy Award for one of his many skilled performances in films, especially when considering the actors who have won awards for performances of no particular distinction. In 1970, by way of compensation, the Academy of Motion Picture Arts and Sciences awarded him a special Oscar, "for being Cary Grant." Following a well-chosen montage of Grant film clips, Frank Sinatra presented him with the special award. Noticeably older, grayer, and heavier, Grant appeared very touched by the tribute.

To all intents, Cary Grant has finally retired. But another Cary Grant never will: the incredibly handsome, dapper, affable, and gifted actor who survived thirty-four years of changing trends and times, is still there on the screen to enchant filmgoers of every generation.

# THE FILMS OF CARY GRANT

The director's name follows the release date. A (c) following the release date indicates that the film was in color. Sp indicates Screenplay and b/o indicates based/on.

1. THIS IS THE NIGHT. Paramount, 1932. *Frank Tuttle*. Sp: George Marion, Jr., b/o play by Avery Hopwood. Cast: Lily Damita, Charles Ruggles, Roland Young, Thelma Todd, Irving Bacon, Claire Dodd.

2. SINNERS IN THE SUN. Paramount, 1932. *Alexander Hall*. Sp: Vincent Lawrence, Waldemar Young, and Samuel Hoffenstein, b/o story by Mildred Cram. Cast: Carole Lombard, Chester Morris, Adrienne Ames, Alison Skipworth, Walter Byron.

3. MERRILY WE GO TO HELL. Paramount, 1932. *Dorothy Arzner*. Sp: Edwin Justus Mayer, b/o novel by Cleo Lucas. Cast: Fredric March, Sylvia Sidney, Adrianne Allen, Richard "Skeets" Gallagher, Kent Taylor.

4. DEVIL AND THE DEEP. Paramount, 1932. *Marion Gering*. Sp: Benn W. Levy, b/o story by Harry Hervey. Cast: Tallulah Bankhead, Gary Cooper, Charles Laughton, Paul Porcasi, Juliette Compton, Henry Kolker, Kent Taylor.

5. BLONDE VENUS. Paramount, 1932. *Josef von Sternberg*. Sp: Jules Furthman and S.K. Lauren, b/o story by Josef von Sternberg. Cast: Marlene Dietrich, Herbert Marshall, Dickie Moore, Sidney Toler, Cecil Cunningham, Hattie McDaniel.

6. HOT SATURDAY. Paramount, 1932. *William A. Seiter*. Sp: Seton I. Miller, b/o novel by Harvey Fergusson. Cast: Nancy Carroll, Randolph Scott, Edward Woods, Lillian Bond, William Collier Sr., Jane Darwell, Grady Sutton.

7. MADAME BUTTERFLY. Paramount, 1932. *Marion Gering*. Sp: Josephine Lovett and Joseph Moncure March, b/o story by John Luther Long and play by David Belasco. Cast: Sylvia Sidney, Charles Ruggles, Irving Pichel, Helen Jerome Eddy, Sheila Terry.

8. SHE DONE HIM WRONG. Paramount, 1933. *Lowell Sherman*. Sp: Harvey Thew and John Bright, b/o play by Mae West. Cast: Mae West, Gilbert Roland, Noah Beery Sr., Rafaela Ottiano, David Landau, Rochelle Hudson, Owen Moore, Fuzzy Knight, Louise Beavers.

9. THE WOMAN ACCUSED. Paramount, 1933. *Paul Sloane*. Sp: Bayard Veiller, b/o magazine serial by Polan Banks, Rupert Hughes, Vicki Baum, Zane Grey, Viña Delmar, Irvin S. Cobb, Gertrude Atherton, J.P. McEvoy, Ursula Parrott, and Sophie Kerr. Cast: Nancy Carroll, John Halliday, Irving Pichel, Louis Calhern, Jack La Rue, John Lodge.

10. THE EAGLE AND THE HAWK. Paramount, 1933. *Stuart Walker*. Sp: Bogart Rogers and Seton I. Miller, b/o story by John Monk Saunders. Cast: Fredric March, Jack Oakie, Carole Lombard, Sir Guy Standing.

11. GAMBLING SHIP. Paramount, 1933. *Louis Gasnier* and *Max Marcin*. Sp: Max Marcin and Seton I. Miller, b/o story by Peter Ruric and adaptation by Claude Binyon. Cast: Benite Hume, Roscoe Karns, Glenda Farrell, Jack La Rue, Arthur Vinton.

12. I'M NO ANGEL. Paramount, 1933. *Wesley Ruggles*. Sp: Mae West and Lowell Brentano. Cast: Mae West, Edward Arnold, Ralf Harolde, Russell Hopton, Gertrude Michael, Kent Taylor, Dorothy Peterson, Gregory Ratoff.

13. ALICE IN WONDERLAND. Paramount, 1933. *Norman Z. McLeod*. Sp: Joseph L. Mankiewicz and William Cameron Menzies, b/o story by Lewis Carroll. Cast: Charlotte Henry, Richard Arlen, Gary Cooper, Leon Errol, Louise Fazenda, W.C. Fields, Sterling Holloway, Edward Everett Horton, Baby LeRoy, Mae Marsh, Jack Oakie, Edna May Oliver, May Robson, Charles Ruggles, Alison Skipworth, Ned Sparks, Jacqueline Wells (Julie Bishop).

14. THIRTY-DAY PRINCESS. Paramount, 1934. *Marion Gering*. Sp: Preston Sturges and Frank Partos, b/o story by Clarence Budington Kelland. Cast: Sylvia Sidney, Edward Arnold, Vince Barnett, Henry Stephenson, Edgar Norton.

15. BORN TO BE BAD. United Artists, 1934. *Lowell Sherman*. Sp: Ralph Graves. Cast: Loretta Young, Jackie Kelk, Henry Travers, Russell Hopton, Andrew Tombes, Harry Green, Marion Burns.

16. KISS AND MAKE-UP. Paramount, 1934. *Harlan Thompson*. Sp: Harlan Thompson and George Marion Jr., b/o play by Stephen Bekeffi and adaptation by Jane Hinton. Cast: Genevieve Tobin, Helen Mack, Edward Everett Horton, Mona Maris, Toby Wing, Clara Lou (Ann) Sheridan, Jacqueline Wells (Julie Bishop).

17. LADIES SHOULD LISTEN. Paramount, 1934. *Frank Tuttle*. Sp: Claude Binyon and Frank Butler, b/o play by Guy Bolton and Alfred Savoir. Cast: Frances Drake, Edward Everett Horton, Charles Arnt, Rosita Moreno, Nydia Westman, George Barbier, Clara Lou (Ann) Sheridan.

18. ENTER MADAME. Paramount, 1934. *Elliott Nugent*. Sp: Charles Brackett and Gladys Lehman, b/o play by Gilda Varesi and Dorothea Donn-Byrne. Cast: Elissa Landi, Lynne Overman, Sharon Lynn, Frank Albertson, Cecilia Parker, Clara Lou (Ann) Sheridan.

19. **WINGS IN THE DARK.** Paramount, 1935. *James Flood.* Sp: Jack Kirkland and Frank Partos, b/o story by Neil Shipman and Philip D. Hurn, adapted by Dale Van Every. Cast: Myrna Loy, Roscoe Karns, Hobart Cavanaugh, Dean Jagger, Bert Hanlon, Russell Hopton.

20. **THE LAST OUTPOST.** Paramount, 1935. *Louis Gasnier* and *Charles Barton.* Sp: Philip MacDonald, b/o story by F. Britten Austin and adaptation by Frank Partos and Charles Brackett. Cast: Claude Rains, Gertrude Michael, Kathleen Burke, Colin Tapley.

21. **SYLVIA SCARLETT.** RKO, 1936. *George Cukor.* Sp: Gladys Unger, John Collier, and Mortimer Offner, b/o novel by Compton MacKenzie. Cast: Katharine Hepburn, Brian Aherne, Edmund Gwenn, Natalie Paley, Dennie Moore.

22. **BIG BROWN EYES.** Paramount, 1936. *Raoul Walsh.* Sp: Raoul Walsh and Bert Hanlon, b/o short stories by James Edward Grant. Cast: Joan Bennett, Walter Pidgeon, Isabel Jewell, Lloyd Nolan, Douglas Fowley, Marjorie Gateson, Alan Baxter.

23. **SUZY.** MGM, 1936. *George Fitzmaurice.* Sp: Dorothy Parker, Alan Campbell, Horace Jackson, and Lenore Coffee, b/o novel by Herbert Gorman. Cast: Jean Harlow, Franchot Tone, Lewis Stone, Benita Hume, Inez Courtney, Stanley Morner (Dennis Morgan), Una O'Connor.

24. **WEDDING PRESENT.** Paramount, 1936. *Richard Wallace.* Sp: Joseph Anthony, b/o story by Paul Gallico. Cast: Joan Bennett, George Bancroft, Conrad Nagel, Gene Lockhart, William Demarest, Inez Courtney, Edward Brophy.

25. **THE AMAZING QUEST OF ERNEST BLISS.** Grand National, 1936. *Alfred Zeisler.* Sp: John L. Balderston, b/o story by E. Phillips Oppenheim. Cast: Mary Brian, Peter Gawthorne, Henry Kendall, John Turnbull. Alternate British title: *A Rich Young Man.* Released in the U.S. in 1937 as *Romance and Riches;* later re-released by Astor Pictures as *Amazing Adventure.*

26. **WHEN YOU'RE IN LOVE.** Columbia, 1937. *Robert Riskin.* Sp: Robert Riskin, b/o story by Ethel Hill and Cedric Worth. Cast: Grace Moore, Aline MacMahon, Henry Stephenson, Thomas Mitchell, Catherine Doucet, Luis Alberni, Emma Dunn.

27. **THE TOAST OF NEW YORK.** RKO, 1937. *Rowland V. Lee.* Sp: Dudley Nichols, John Twist, and Joel Sayre, b/o book by Bouck White and story by Matthew Josephson. Cast: Edward Arnold, Frances Farmer, Jack Oakie, Donald Meek, Thelma Leeds, Clarence Kolb, Billy Gilbert.

28. **TOPPER.** MGM, 1937. *Norman Z. McLeod.* Sp: Jack Jevne, Eric Hatch, and Eddie Moran, b/o novel by Thorne Smith. Cast: Constance Bennett, Roland Young, Billie Burke, Alan Mowbray, Eugene Pallette, Arthur Lake, Hedda Hopper, Virginia Sale.

29. THE AWFUL TRUTH. Columbia, 1937. *Leo McCarey*. Sp: Viña Delmar, b/o play by Arthur Richman. Cast: Irene Dunne, Ralph Bellamy, Alexander D'Arcy, Cecil Cunningham, Molly Lamont, Esther Dale, Mary Forbes, and Mr. Smith ("Asta" of the *Thin Man* series). Originally filmed in 1925. Remade in 1953 as *Let's Do It Again*.

30. BRINGING UP BABY. RKO, 1938. *Howard Hawks*. Sp: Dudley Nichols and Hagar Wilde, b/o story by Wilde. Cast: Katharine Hepburn, Charles Ruggles, May Robson, Walter Catlett, Barry Fitzgerald, Fritz Feld, Tala Birell.

31. HOLIDAY. Columbia, 1938. *George Cukor*. Sp: Donald Ogden Stewart and Sidney Buchman, b/o play by Philip Barry. Cast: Katharine Hepburn, Doris Nolan, Lew Ayres, Edward Everett Horton, Henry Kolker, Jean Dixon, Binnie Barnes, Henry Daniell, Bess Flowers. Also filmed in 1930.

32. GUNGA DIN. RKO, 1939. *George Stevens*. Sp: Joel Sayre and Fred Guiol, b/o story by Ben Hecht and Charles MacArthur, suggested by the Rudyard Kipling poem. Cast: Victor McLaglen, Douglas Fairbanks Jr., Eduardo Ciannelli, Joan Fontaine, Montagu Love, Sam Jaffe.

33. ONLY ANGELS HAVE WINGS. Columbia, 1939. *Howard Hawks*. Sp: Jules Furthman, b/o story by Howard Hawks. Cast: Jean Arthur, Richard Barthelmess, Rita Hayworth, Thomas Mitchell, Sig Ruman, Victor Kilian, John Carroll, Allyn Joslyn, Donald Barry, Noah Beery Jr.

34. IN NAME ONLY. RKO, 1939. *John Cromwell*. Sp: Richard Sherman, b/o novel by Bessie Breuer. Cast: Carole Lombard, Kay Francis, Charles Coburn, Helen Vinson, Katharine Alexander, Jonathan Hale, Peggy Ann Garner.

35. HIS GIRL FRIDAY. Columbia, 1940. *Howard Hawks*. Sp: Charles Lederer, b/o play by Ben Hecht and Charles MacArthur. Cast: Rosalind Russell, Ralph Bellamy, Gene Lockhart, Porter Hall, Ernest Truex, Cliff Edwards, Clarence Kolb, Roscoe Karns, Frank Jenks, Regis Toomey, John Qualen, Helen Mack, Alma Kruger, Billy Gilbert, Marion Martin. Remake of *The Front Page* (1931).

36. MY FAVORITE WIFE. RKO, 1940. *Garson Kanin*. Sp: Bella and Samuel Spewack, b/o story by the Spewacks and Leo McCarey. Cast: Irene Dunne, Randolph Scott, Gail Patrick, Ann Shoemaker, Scotty Beckett, Donald MacBride, Granville Bates. Remade in 1963 as *Move Over, Darling*. (The ill-fated 1962 remake, entitled *Something's Got to Give*, was abandoned with the death of its star, Marilyn Monroe.)

37. THE HOWARDS OF VIRGINIA. Columbia, 1940. *Frank Lloyd*. Sp: Sidney Buchman, b/o novel by Elizabeth Page. Cast: Martha Scott, Sir Cedric Hardwicke, Alan Marshal, Richard Carlson, Paul Kelly, Irving Bacon, Elisabeth Risdon, Anne Revere, Richard Alden (Tom Drake).

**38. THE PHILADELPHIA STORY. MGM, 1940. *George Cukor*. Sp: Donald Ogden Stewart, b/o play by Philip Barry. Cast: Katharine Hepburn, James Stewart, Ruth Hussey, John Howard, Roland Young, John Halliday, Virginia Weidler, Mary Nash, Henry Daniell. Remade in 1956 as musical *High Society*.**

**39. PENNY SERENADE. Columbia, 1941. *George Stevens*. Sp: Morrie Ryskind, b/o story by Martha Cheavens. Cast: Irene Dunne, Beulah Bondi, Edgar Buchanan, Ann Doran, Eva Lee Kuney.**

**40. SUSPICION. RKO, 1941. *Alfred Hitchcock*. Sp: Samson Raphaelson, Joan Harrison, and Alma Reville, b/o novel by Francis Iles. Cast: Joan Fontaine, Sir Cedric Hardwicke, Nigel Bruce, Dame May Whitty, Isabel Jeans, Heather Angel, Leo G. Carroll.**

**41. THE TALK OF THE TOWN. Columbia, 1942. *George Stevens*. Sp: Irwin Shaw and Sidney Buchman. Cast: Jean Arthur, Ronald Colman, Edgar Buchanan, Glenda Farrell, Charles Dingle, Emma Dunn, Rex Ingram.**

**42. ONCE UPON A HONEYMOON. RKO, 1942. *Leo McCarey*. Sp: Sheridan Gibney, b/o story by Gibney and Leo McCarey. Cast: Ginger Rogers, Walter Slezak, Albert Dekker, Albert Basserman, Ferike Boros.**

**43. MR. LUCKY. RKO, 1943. *H.C. Potter*. Sp: Milton Holmes and Adrian Scott. Cast: Laraine Day, Charles Bickford, Gladys Cooper, Alan Carney, Henry Stephenson, Paul Stewart, Kay Johnson, Walter Kingsford, J.M. Kerrigan, Vladimir Sokoloff, Florence Bates.**

**44. DESTINATION TOKYO. Warners, 1944. *Delmer Daves*. Sp: Delmer Daves and Albert Maltz, b/o story by Steve Fisher. Cast: John Garfield, Alan Hale, John Ridgely, Dane Clark, Warner Anderson, William Prince, Robert Hutton, Tom Tully, Faye Emerson, John Forsythe.**

**45. ONCE UPON A TIME. Columbia, 1944. *Alexander Hall*. Sp: Lewis Meltzer and Oscar Paul, b/o adaptation by Irving Fineman of story by Norman Corwin and Lucille Fletcher Herrmann. Cast: Janet Blair, James Gleason, Ted Donaldson, Howard Freeman, William Demarest.**

**46. ARSENIC AND OLD LACE. Warners, 1944. *Frank Capra*. Sp: Julius J. and Philip G. Epstein, b/o play by Joseph Kesselring. Cast: Priscilla Lane, Raymond Massey, Josephine Hull, Jean Adair, Jack Carson, Edward Everett Horton, Peter Lorre, James Gleason, John Alexander, Grant Mitchell.**

**47. NONE BUT THE LONELY HEART. RKO, 1944. *Clifford Odets*. Sp: Odets, b/o novel by Richard Llewellyn. Cast: Ethel Barrymore, Barry Fitzgerald, June Duprez, Jane Wyatt, George Coulouris, Dan Duryea, Roman Bohnen.**

**48. NIGHT AND DAY. Warners, 1946. (c) *Michael Curtiz*. Sp: Charles Hoffman, Leo Townsend, and William Bowers, b/o career of Cole Porter. Cast: Alexis Smith, Monty Woolley, Ginny Simms, Jane Wyman, Eve Arden, Victor Francen, Alan Hale, Dorothy Malone, Selena Royle, Mary Martin.**

49. NOTORIOUS. RKO, 1946. *Alfred Hitchcock*. Sp: Ben Hecht. Cast: Ingrid Bergman, Claude Rains, Louis Calhern, Mme. Leopoldine Konstantin, Ivan Triesault, Reinhold Schunzel, Moroni Olsen.

50. THE BACHELOR AND THE BOBBY-SOXER. RKO, 1947. *Irving Reis*. Sp: Sidney Sheldon. Cast: Myrna Loy, Shirley Temple, Rudy Vallee, Ray Collins, Harry Davenport, Johnny Sands, Don Beddoe, Veda Ann Borg.

51. THE BISHOP'S WIFE. RKO, 1947. *Henry Koster*. Sp: Robert E. Sherwood and Leonardo Bercovici, b/o novel by Robert Nathan. Cast: Loretta Young, David Niven, Monty Woolley, James Gleason, Gladys Cooper, Elsa Lanchester, Sara Haden.

52. MR. BLANDINGS BUILDS HIS DREAM HOUSE. RKO, 1948. *H.C. Potter*. Sp: Norman Panama and Melvin Frank, b/o novel by Eric Hodgins. Cast: Myrna Loy, Melvyn Douglas, Sharyn Moffett, Connie Marshall, Louise Beavers, Lurene Tuttle, Reginald Denny.

53. EVERY GIRL SHOULD BE MARRIED. RKO, 1948. *Don Hartman*. Sp: Hartman and Stephen Morehouse Avery, b/o story by Eleanor Harris. Cast: Betsy Drake, Franchot Tone, Diana Lynn, Eddie Albert, Elisabeth Risdon, Alan Mowbray.

54. I WAS A MALE WAR BRIDE. 20th Century-Fox, 1949. *Howard Hawks*. Sp: Charles Lederer, Leonard Spigelgass, and Hagar Wilde, b/o story by Henri Rochard. Cast: Ann Sheridan, William Neff, Eugene Gericke, Marion Marshall, Randy Stuart.

55. CRISIS. MGM, 1950. *Richard Brooks*. Sp: Brooks, b/o story by George Tabori. Cast: Jose Ferrer, Paula Raymond, Signe Hasso, Ramon Novarro, Gilbert Roland, Antonio Moreno, Leon Ames, Teresa Celli.

56. PEOPLE WILL TALK. 20th Century-Fox, 1951. *Joseph L. Mankiewicz*. Sp: Mankiewicz, b/o play by Curt Goetz. Cast: Jeanne Crain, Finlay Currie, Hume Cronyn, Walter Slezak, Sidney Blackmer, Katherine Locke, Will Wright, Margaret Hamilton. Remake of the 1933 German film, *Dr. Praetorious*.

57. ROOM FOR ONE MORE. Warners, 1952. *Norman Taurog*. Sp: Melville Shavelson and Jack Rose, b/o book by Anna Perrott Rose. Cast: Betsy Drake, Iris Mann, George Winslow, Clifford Tatum Jr., Gay Gordon, Malcolm Cassell, Larry Olsen, Lurene Tuttle.

58. MONKEY BUSINESS. 20th Century-Fox, 1952. *Howard Hawks*. Sp: I.A.L. Diamond, Charles Lederer, and Ben Hecht. Cast: Ginger Rogers, Charles Coburn, Marilyn Monroe, Hugh Marlowe, Henri Letondal, Larry Keating, Esther Dale, George Winslow.

59. DREAM WIFE. MGM, 1953. *Sidney Sheldon*. Sp: Sidney Sheldon, Herbert Baker, and Alfred Lewis Levitt. Cast: Deborah Kerr, Walter Pidgeon, Betta St. John, Eduard Franz, Buddy Baer, Les Tremayne, Bruce Bennett.

60. **TO CATCH A THIEF.** Paramount, 1955. (c) *Alfred Hitchcock*. Sp: John Michael Hayes, b/o novel by David Dodge. Cast: Grace Kelly, Jessie Royce Landis, John Williams, Charles Vanel, Brigitte Auber, Jean Martinelli.

61. **THE PRIDE AND THE PASSION.** United Artists, 1957. (c) *Stanley Kramer*. Sp: Edna and Edward Anhalt, b/o novel by C.S. Forester. Cast: Frank Sinatra, Sophia Loren, Theodore Bikel, John Wengraf, Jay Novello.

62. **AN AFFAIR TO REMEMBER.** 20th Century-Fox, 1957. (c) *Leo McCarey*. Sp: Delmer Daves and Leo McCarey, b/o original story by McCarey and Mildred Cram. Cast: Deborah Kerr, Richard Denning, Neva Patterson, Cathleen Nesbitt, Robert Q. Lewis. Remake of the 1939 Charles Boyer-Irene Dunne *Love Affair*.

63. **KISS THEM FOR ME.** 20th Century-Fox, 1957. (c) *Stanley Donen*. Sp: Julius J. Epstein, b/o play by Luther Davis and novel by Frederic Wakeman. Cast: Jayne Mansfield, Leif Erickson, Suzy Parker, Ray Walston, Larry Blyden, Nathaniel Frey, Werner Klemperer, Jack Mullaney.

64. **INDISCREET.** Warners, 1958. (c) *Stanley Donen*. Sp: Norman Krasna, b/o his play. Cast: Ingrid Bergman, Cecil Parker, Phyllis Calvert, David Kossoff, Megs Jenkins, Oliver Johnston.

65. **HOUSEBOAT.** Paramount, 1958. (c) *Melville Shavelson*. Sp: Melville Shavelson and Jack Rose. Cast: Sophia Loren, Martha Hyer, Charles Herbert, Mimi Gibson, Paul Petersen, Eduardo Ciannelli, Harry Guardino, Murray Hamilton.

66. **NORTH BY NORTHWEST.** MGM, 1959. (c) *Alfred Hitchcock*. Sp: Ernest Lehman. Cast: Eva Marie Saint, James Mason, Jessie Royce Landis, Leo G. Carroll, Philip Ober, Josephine Hutchinson, Martin Landau, Adam Williams, Edward Platt.

67. **OPERATION PETTICOAT.** Universal, 1959. (c) *Blake Edwards*. Sp: Stanley Shapiro and Maurice Richlin, b/o story by Paul King and Joseph Stone. Cast: Tony Curtis, Joan O'Brien, Dina Merrill, Arthur O'Connell, Gene Evans, Richard Sargent, Virginia Gregg, Robert F. Simon.

68. **THE GRASS IS GREENER.** Universal, 1960. (c) *Stanley Donen*. Sp: Hugh and Margaret Williams, b/o their play. Cast: Deborah Kerr, Robert Mitchum, Jean Simmons, Moray Watson.

69. **THAT TOUCH OF MINK.** Universal, 1962. (c) *Delbert Mann*. Sp: Stanley Shapiro and Nate Monaster. Cast: Doris Day, Gig Young, Audrey Meadows, Alan Hewitt, John Astin, Richard Sargent, Joey Faye.

70. **CHARADE.** Universal, 1963. (c) *Stanley Donen*. Sp: Peter Stone and Marc Behm. Cast: Audrey Hepburn, Walter Matthau, James Coburn, George Kennedy, Ned Glass, Jacques Marin.

71. **FATHER GOOSE.** Universal, 1964. (c) *Ralph Nelson*. Sp: Peter Stone and Frank Tarloff, b/o story by S.H. Barnett. Cast: Leslie Caron, Trevor Howard, Jack Good, Stephanie Berrington, Jennifer Berrington.

72. WALK, DON'T RUN. Columbia, 1966. (c) *Charles Walters*. Sp: Sol Saks, b/o story by Robert Russell and Frank Ross. Cast: Samantha Eggar, Jim Hutton, John Standing, Miiko Taka, Ted Hartley. Remake of *The More the Merrier* (1943).

---

Cary Grant also made brief, unbilled screen appearances in the following films:

1. SINGAPORE SUE. Par., 1932. CG and Millard Mitchell had supporting roles as sailors in this musical short starring Anna Chang.

2. HOLLYWOOD ON PARADE. Par., 1932-1934. CG was among the many stars who appeared as themselves in this series of 10-minute shorts. In one entry, he plays straight man to a youngster's hilarious imitation of Mae West.

3. PIRATE PARTY ON CATALINA ISLAND. MGM, 1936. CG joined Errol Flynn, John Gilbert, Lee Tracy, and other stars in this 20-minute color short.

4. THE ROAD TO VICTORY. WB, 1944. CG and Jack Carson were among the stars in this one-reel salute to the war effort.

5. WITHOUT RESERVATIONS. RKO, 1946. CG appeared briefly as himself, dancing with Claudette Colbert in this comedy costarring Colbert with John Wayne.

6. ELVIS—THAT'S THE WAY IT IS. MGM, 1970. CG, Juliet Prowse, Xavier Cugat, and Sammy Davis Jr. were among the celebrities appearing as themselves in this color documentary about an Elvis Presley concert in Las Vegas.

# BIBLIOGRAPHY

.Baxter, John. *The Cinema of Josef von Sternberg*. A. Zwemmer, London, 1971.

Blum, Daniel. *A Pictorial History of the American Theatre: 1860-1970*. Crown Publishers, New York, 1971.

Bogdanovich, Peter. *The Cinema of Alfred Hitchcock*. The Museum of Modern Art Film Library, distributed by Doubleday, Garden City, New York, 1963.

Capra, Frank. *The Name Above the Title*. The Macmillan Co., New York, 1971.

Carey, Gary. *Cukor & Co*. The Museum of Modern Art, New York, 1971.

Conway, Michael and Ricci, Mark. *The Films of Jean Harlow*. The Citadel Press, New York, 1965.

Dickens, Homer. *The Films of Gary Cooper*. The Citadel Press, New York, 1970.

Farmer, Frances. *Will There Really Be a Morning?* G.P. Putnam's Sons, New York, 1972.

Govoni, Albert. *Cary Grant: An Unauthorized Biography*. Henry Regnery Co., Chicago, 1971.

Gow, Gordon. *Hollywood in the Fifties*. A.S. Barnes & Co., New York, 1971.

Greene, Graham. *Graham Greene on Film*. Simon & Schuster, Inc., New York, 1972.

Griffith, Richard. *Frank Capra*. The British Film Institute, London, 1950.

Griffith, Richard and Mayer, Arthur. *The Movies*. Simon & Schuster Inc., New York, 1957.

Gussow, Mel. *Don't Say Yes Until I Finish Talking*. Doubleday & Co., Inc., New York, 1971.

Hagen, Ray. *Ann Sheridan Interview*. Screen Facts #14, 1966.

Kael, Pauline. *Kiss Kiss Bang Bang*. Atlantic-Little Brown, Boston, 1968.

Maltin, Leonard. *The Great Movie Shorts*. Crown Publishers, New York, 1972.

Mantle, Burns. *The Best Plays of 1920-1921*. Dodd, Mead and Co., New York, 1921.

Mantle, Burns. *The Best Plays of 1927-1928*. Dodd, Mead and Co., New York, 1928.

Mantle, Burns. *The Best Plays of 1928-1929*. Dodd, Mead and Co., New York, 1929.

Mantle, Burns. *The Best Plays of 1929-1930*. Dodd, Mead and Co., New York, 1930.

Mantle, Burns. *The Best Plays of 1931-1932*. Dodd, Mead and Co., New York, 1932.

Mayersberg, Paul. *Hollywood the Haunted House*. Stein and Day, New York, 1968.

Meyer, Jim. *Deborah Kerr* article. Screen Facts #19, 1968.

Michael, Paul. *The American Movies Reference Book*. Prentice-Hall, Englewood, New Jersey, 1969.

Newquist, Roy M. *A Special Kind of Magic*. Rand McNally & Co., Chicago, Illinois, 1967.

Ott, Frederick W. *The Films of Carole Lombard*. The Citadel Press, Secaucus, New Jersey, 1972.

Parish, James Robert. *The Paramount Pretties*. Arlington House, New Rochelle, New York, 1972.

Perry, George. *The Films of Alfred Hitchcock*. Studio Vista, London, 1965.

Quigley, Martin Jr. and Gertner, Richard. *Films in America: 1929-1969*. Golden Press, New York, 1970.

Quirk, Lawrence J. *The Films of Ingrid Bergman*. The Citadel Press, New York, 1970.

Quirk, Lawrence J. *The Films of Fredric March*. The Citadel Press, New York, 1971.

Richie, Donald. *George Stevens: An American Romantic*. The Museum of Modern Art, New York, 1970.

Ringgold, Gene and McCarty, Clifford. *The Films of Frank Sinatra*. The Citadel Press, New York, 1971.

Rivkin, Allen and Kerr, Laura. *Hello, Hollywood!* Doubleday & Co., Inc., New York, 1962.

Roman, Robert C. *Cary Grant*. Films in Review, December, 1961.

Sarris, Andrew. *The Films of Josef von Sternberg*. The Museum of Modern Art, New York, 1966.

Sarris, Andrew. *Interviews with Film Directors*. The Bobbs-Merrill Co., Inc., New York, 1967.

Sennett, Ted. *Warner Brothers Presents*. Arlington House, New York, 1971.

Taylor, John Russell. *Cinema Eye, Cinema Ear*. Hill & Wang, New York, 1964.

Truffaut, Francois. *Hitchcock*. Simon and Schuster, New York, 1966.

Von Sternberg, Josef. *Fun in a Chinese Laundry*. The Macmillan Co., New York, 1965.

Wald, Jerry and Macauley, Richard. *The Best Pictures: 1939-1940*. Dodd, Mead & Co., New York, 1940.

Wood, Robin. *Howard Hawks*. Doubleday & Co., Inc., Garden City, New York, 1968.

# INDEX

*(Page numbers italicized indicate photographs)*

155

159